BEAUTY

A PATH TO GOD

ANTHONY J. CIORRA

Paulist Press
New York / Mahwah, NJ

Cover image by Tischenko Irina / Shutterstock.com
Cover and book design by Sharyn Banks

Library of Congress Cataloging-in-Publication Data

Ciorra, Anthony J.
    Beauty : a path to God / Anthony J. Ciorra.
        pages cm
    Includes bibliographical references.
    ISBN 978-0-8091-4831-8 (alk. paper) — ISBN 978-1-58768-240-7
1. Balthasar, Hans Urs von, 1905–1988. 2. Christianity and the arts.
3. Aesthetics—Religious aspects—Christianity. I. Title.
    BR115.A8C56 2013
    261.5`7—dc23

                                                                2012046221

ISBN: 978-0-8091-4831-8 (paperback)
ISBN: 978-1-58768-240-7 (e-book)

Published by Paulist Press
997 Macarthur Boulevard

Mahwah, New Jersey 07430

www.paulistpress.com

Printed and bound in the
United States of America

"ALL HUMAN NATURE VIGOROUSLY RESISTS GRACE BECAUSE
GRACE CHANGES US AND THE CHANGE IS PAINFUL."
Flannery O'Connor, *The Habit of Being*

In thanksgiving for two ministers of God's beauty:
Saint John XXIII (1881–1963) and
Thomas Merton (1915–1968),
who have shown us how to courageously resist
fear and vigorously embrace grace.

CONTENTS

CONTENTS

ACKNOWLEDGMENTS

No one learns alone and no one writes a book alone. I am grateful for the support that I have received from so many people during the evolution of this book on beauty.

I give thanks to the One who is the source of all that is beautiful and hope that this book will draw others into the beauty of God's love.

I am inspired by the vision of Fr. Mark-David Janus and the staff at Paulist Press. The contribution of the Press to the academy, Church, and society is monumental. I am especially grateful to Nancy de Flon, my editor at Paulist Press. Nancy has challenged me with her insights, suggestions, and above all her wisdom.

I met Catherine Strader from Our Lady of the Lake Parish, Verona, New Jersey, on Pentecost Sunday, 2012. She has been a gift of the Spirit in my life and in the writing of this book. Her suggestions, brilliance, and mind for detail have been invaluable in bringing this book to completion.

I am especially grateful to my family for their encouragement, support, and love. My mother often reminded me, "You should be grateful, for you have a wonderful family." I *am* grateful and have been blessed by the goodness and inspiration of my family. They mirror God's beauty in my life.

I am also grateful for my spiritual family, the Voluntas Dei Institute, for affirming me and challenging me to use my gifts for the service of the Church and the world.

Thank-you to my colleagues and friends who have offered invaluable suggestions and advice, especially Margaret Gardner, Robert Clark, Dr. Michael Higgins, Dr. David Coppola, Dr. June-Ann Greeley, Dr. Nathan Lewis, and Dr. Gloria Durka.

Finally, a thank-you to Dr. John Petillo and the Sacred Heart University administration, faculty, staff, and students for affirming scholarship, encouraging creativity, and fostering a culture of friendship and kindness that makes the university a place where the love of God and the love of learning flourish.

AN INTRODUCTION
TO BEAUTY

The world, the country, and the Church are entering uncharted territory in the twenty-first century. The premise of this book is that beauty is the gateway to a new spirituality for this new century. Beauty draws from eternal truths and translates these for the contemporary world. This book explores a spirituality of beauty that respects yet builds on the tradition of Christian spirituality.

In the fourth century, when St. Augustine struggled with the allurements of the pleasures encouraged by pagan philosophy, he was not afraid to remain open to the questions arising from the juxtaposition of paganism with the early Christian teachings. Eventually, truth and beauty prevailed through the instrumentality of his mother's prayers and the preaching of St. Ambrose. In his *Confessions*, St. Augustine wrote that God, as Beauty, was the source of all earthly beauty.

> Late have I loved you, Beauty ever ancient and ever
>   new,
> Late have I loved you!
> Lo, you were within,
> But I outside, seeking there for you.
> You called, shouted, broke through my deafness;
> You flared, blazed, banished my blindness;
> You lavished your fragrance, I gasped, and now I pant
>   for you;
> I tasted you, and I hunger and thirst;
> You touched me, and I burned for your peace.[1]

Seventeen centuries later, we face similar allurements from a secular culture that raise new questions. What St. Augustine did in the fourth century is what we need to do in the twenty-first century. The God that lured St. Augustine through beauty will do the same for today's seekers, if we have the courage to stay the course. Beauty will again prevail. St. Augustine's experience can become ours.

Artistic images of St. Augustine depict him as holding his heart in his hand. Today, we would say that he is wearing his heart on his sleeve. A spirituality of beauty is one that begins with the heart. The beauty that is *ever ancient* allures us to new spiritual paths in today's world. Technology, globalization, and new spiritualities are not our enemies but rather vehicles toward new definitions of beauty. The pursuit of beauty unites us in a common quest to discover what it means to be human in this new epoch. In his *Letter to Artists*, Pope John Paul II described the work of artists as "epiphanies of beauty" and urged them to share this beauty with the world through their art. The pope understood that today's changing needs demand new epiphanies, new ways of creating beauty that will bring us into the mystery of God's love. The twenty-first century needs women and men who bring an understanding of the mystical tradition coupled with an openness to integrating this tradition into their contemporary lives. We need artisans of the spiritual life who can find the beauty within their hearts and bring that beauty into the world. Just as the Renaissance was a watershed moment for religious art, today's new quest for spirituality is a blank canvas for those willing to stroke the brush. Our task will be to remind the world how beautiful it is. The "I want spirituality but not religion" mantra of today's culture points to the fact that there is an emptiness in the human soul that is crying out for the mystical presence of God and is not being met by the ancient ways of the spiritual tradition. Today's artists of the spiritual life are those who will creatively use the gift of beauty to close the gap between religion and spirituality.

Dostoevsky, in his novel *The Idiot,* gives a hint as to how this needs to be done: "Is it true, prince, that you once declared that beauty would save the world?"[2] Although a lasting spirituality must be rooted in good theology, its focus is not on explaining doctrines but on transforming lives. The poetry and song about a loving God will touch hearts. Beauty will save the world by joining religion and spirituality.

Prayer is making space available for God to do beautiful things with your life. St. Luke uses the example of Mary, who "treasured all these words and pondered them in her heart" (Luke 2:19). It is noteworthy that the locus of her pondering is in the heart. She does not begin in her head. The Greek notion *to ponder* was to think through all the angles. This was the method of the great philosophers, such as Plato and Aristotle. For the Hebrew mind, *to ponder* was not about thinking but about being transformed. The Jewish concept of pondering was to hold contradictions and uncertainties in tension within the human heart. Final answers and certainties do not produce beauty. The choice to stay with the questions allows beauty to emerge at its own pace. To rush beauty, to run ahead of grace, is to squelch it. To pray is to stay with the tension of birthing in the midst of emptiness.

In his *Letter to Artists*, Pope John Paul II described this dynamic, quoting the Polish poet Adam Mickiewicz: "From chaos rises the world of the spirit."[3] The pope concluded, "May your art help to affirm that true beauty which, as a glimmer of the Spirit of God, will transfigure matter, opening the human soul to the sense of the eternal." Alexander Solzhenitsyn described the powerful spirituality that is stimulated by art in his 1970 Nobel Prize acceptance speech: "Art inflames even a frozen, darkened soul to a high spiritual experience."

It is the Spirit of God who brings us to the feast of beauty. The very same Spirit that breathed over the chaos in the Book of Genesis continues to create beauty from the chaos of our lives. The Spirit is the holy artist who creates beauty in the midst of mystery. The Spirit, who makes our imperfect prayer perfect, is the One who creates beauty from the brokenness of our lives. St. Paul writes, "The Spirit helps us in our weakness; for we do not know how to pray as we ought, but that very Spirit intercedes with sighs too deep for words. And God, who searches the heart, knows what is the mind of the Spirit" (Rom 8:26–27). The Spirit gives us a courageous vision that connects the human spirit with the divine fire of love.

It is precisely through prayer that the Spirit connects our hearts with the One for whom we long. God commissions us through the Spirit to craft our lives into a masterpiece that will draw others to the Beautiful One. Indeed, we are ministers of God's beauty. The Japanese have an expression, "Do not mistake the pointing finger for the moon." We are the *finger* that God makes beautiful so that we can attract others to him.

The fathers of the Second Vatican Council listened to seven speeches given at the conclusion of the Council on December 8, 1965. One of the speeches was addressed to artists. The speech commissions us to bring a spirituality of beauty into the twenty-first century, pointing out, "It is beauty, like truth, which brings joy to the heart of the human person" and urging today's artists to serve as "the guardians of beauty in the world."

The Council fathers warn us to beware of "tastes that are passing." A spirituality that will be *ever new* must be built on a tradition that is *ever ancient*. The Christian writer Evelyn Underhill espouses a mysticism that is practical rather than theoretical. She suggests rites of passage for achieving the goal of love through the development of human consciousness, beginning with an awakening and followed by purgation, illumination, darkness, and union.[4] She taught that the first and most important rite of passage is to wake up to the presence of the divine. We need to open our eyes and see anew what was always there but we never noticed.

This book explores the ability of beauty, and of the process of searching for and appreciating the beauty of God's world, to introduce components of prayer, joy, and spirituality into our lives today. We start by looking broadly at the spirituality that comes from living amidst beauty and then focus on the beauty that resides in key aspects of a strong spiritual life, exploring the beauty inherent in appreciating the present moment, the beauty associated with forgiveness, and the beauty that comes from gratitude. Finally, we end with an exploration of darkness as the path to beauty, understanding that great beauty often has its origins in times of spiritual or emotional darkness and melancholy.

This book is an invitation to embrace a spirituality of beauty. Many of the visual and verbal works of art cited in the text are listed at the back of the book in "Web Site References," which gives a Web address at which the works can be viewed or read online. Take the time to experience these works firsthand and linger in their beauty. At the end of each chapter, I leave you with suggestions for further reflection and invite you to reflect, discuss, and experience these with others as you continue on the road to beauty. Works of beauty are best appreciated when two or three are gathered. The deep knowledge that we call wisdom can only happen in the context of a community; we cannot know alone. The disciples on the road to Emmaus became a community of beauty when they opened their eyes together in the presence of God's risen beauty.

Once we are touched by beauty, we begin to notice the ways in which we need to be transformed. We are purified of those things that prevent us from experiencing beauty and from becoming beautiful. It is at this point that the light begins to come through the cracks. Grace is the creative energy that facilitates change. This energy blows like the wind and pushes us into the desert. It is here that the Divine Artist chisels away to create a masterpiece, like Michelangelo carving his *Pietà* from a deformed piece of marble. Finally, the journey ends in ecstasy in the arms of the Divine Artist. In that moment, we no longer pray but become a prayer. We are transformed by beauty to offer a new path to God in the twenty-first century.

CHAPTER ONE

ART AND THE BEAUTY OF SPIRITUALITY

SEEING COLORS

The springboard for the spirituality of beauty in this book borrows from the letter of Pope John Paul II to artists.[1] Since the pope was also a poet, this particular piece was written from his personal experience of being transformed by beauty. He makes a bold and clear assertion when he writes, "None can see more deeply than you artists, ingenious creatures that you are, something of the pathos with which God, at the dawn of creation, looked upon the work of divine hands" (§1). In this letter, he marvels at the ability of artists to create beauty from elements unseen or unappreciated by others. He compares the sense of satisfaction felt by artists to God's response to the artistry of the newly created world, "indeed, it was very good" (Gen 1:31). The eyes are the mirrors of the soul. It is the Spirit that creates this glimmer that is pure gift and that overflows into colors and sounds as if to create a new Pentecost. This transformation is reminiscent of the scene from the movie *The Wizard of Oz*, in which Dorothy approaches a house that is "black and white" on the outside. When she opens the door, she is overwhelmed by colors.[2] Similarly, the Spirit brings us out of a black and white world into the room of God's heart that is filled with colors.

We spend most of the liturgical year in Ordinary Time. It is the Spirit who makes ordinary time truly extraordinary. The saints and mystics over the centuries have used the image of light to express their experience of the Spirit, who brings brilliance out of the darkness of the ordinary. Touched by the Spirit, the human journey occurs in a universe ablaze with colors. Building upon Karl Rahner's concept of the *anonymous Christian*, I purport that there are artists by charism and trade and then there are *anonymous artists*. Every human being is an artist at heart, having been created in the image and likeness of God. If we live with that realization, all that we do is a work of art as we transform the ordinariness of daily life with the brush of God's grace. What the pope wrote to those who are artists by trade can be applied to the artist that lives in every human being. He writes to all of us, "A glimmer of that feeling has shown so often in your eyes when, like the artists of every age…captivated by the hidden power of sounds and words, colors and shapes, you have admired the work of your inspiration, sensing in it some echo of the mystery of creation with which God, the sole creator of all things, has wished in some way to associate with you" (§1).

There is something wonderful happening in the world. We are being formed into craftspersons who share with others "what we have heard, what we have seen with our eyes, what we have looked at and touched with our hands" (1 John 1:1). Others want to have a taste of the beauty they see in those who are led by the Spirit. The human family is gradually emerging as a community of craftspersons.

This community formed by the Spirit is not obsessed with beauty as an end in itself. Rather, it sees beauty as a gateway to a way of life that reflects the rays of goodness. There is an intimate connection between beauty and the good. In fact, Pope John Paul II points out that the Greeks fused the two concepts, forming the new word *kalokagathia*, which translates as "beauty-goodness" (§3). We become *kalokagathia* when the actions of our lives demonstrate the charity that is the fruit of a true appreciation of beauty. The goodness of God is expressed in our world when we treat others with the beauty of charity. This challenge places us on the battleground where the struggle between good and evil occurs. Each day in which we choose the good through kindness and compassion we bring color into our world.

Jesus became human to draw us into beauty by his life and teachings. A spirituality of beauty is about becoming like the human Christ. Pope John Paul II reminds us in his letter that the gospel message is replete with beautiful stories, scenes, words, and images of the incarnate Jesus, the Son of God, giving us a rich reservoir of what is true and good for our own transformation. He expressed this when he wrote, "In becoming human, the Son of God has introduced into human history all the evangelical wealth of the true and the good. With this, he has unveiled a new dimension of beauty of which the gospel message is filled to the brim" (§5).

THE SYMPHONY OF THE WORD

The scriptures are God's love letters to us that are filled with exquisite beauty. For this reason, the Jewish rabbis would cover its pages with honey and kiss the pages so that the words of beauty would also become beauty in the human heart. We receive the beauty of God's message in the written word and we invite others into this beauty. The same Spirit who inspired the writers of scripture with beautiful thoughts also inspires the readers of scripture with its beauty.

Franciscan preaching in the Middle Ages emerged from this paradigm. The way of preaching adapted by St. Francis and his followers was one that set the sacred to music. Called *Laudes* from the Latin word for "praises," this preaching or praise invited all who were listening to join in the song of God's children. Poetry and song, not prosaic sermons, were used to paint the scene of the heavenly banquet.

Reading the scriptures is not about absorbing a collection of words. It is about becoming absorbed in God. The Jewish people would first wash their hands as a sign of reverence and respect to prepare for an encounter with the word. They looked beyond the surface of the text. *Midrash* is the word they coined to describe this way of approaching the sacred texts. There were two kinds of *midrash*: *midrash halakhah*, which were legal rulings, and *midrash haggadah*, which were elaborations on a story in order to accentuate special teachings about beauty.

For example, in the Gospels, the lawyer asks a question of *halakhah*, "Which commandment is the first of all?" (Mark 12:28). Jesus replies by quoting two paragraphs from the law: "You shall love the Lord your God with all your heart, and with all your soul, and with all your might" (Deut 6:5) and "...you shall love your neighbor as yourself" (Lev 19:18). In Mark's Gospel, Jesus went far beyond the standard answer by bracketing these two commandments into one. He created a new work of beauty by joining these separate texts to mean something radically new. In this revolutionary teaching, love of God is equated with love of neighbor. We no longer have two separate teachings but one new work of beauty that would change the world.

The same is true of Jesus' teaching about the Sabbath. The Sabbath is one of the principle provisions of the law, and so Jesus does not negate it—rather, he revitalizes it into a work of beauty rather than the fulfillment of juridical obligations. First, he subordinates its observance to a deeper level that invites his listeners into a new reality: "The sabbath was made for humankind, and not humankind for the sabbath" (Mark 2:27). Second, he makes a clear statement about who he is and what his mission is when he concludes, "The Son of Man is lord even of the sabbath" (Mark 2:28).

The scriptures will transform our lives if we are able to see beyond words on a page. We must persevere to move beyond the first level of naiveté, in which we see only the surface, to the second level of naiveté, in which we see beneath the surface. It is this second naiveté that is necessary to move beyond the text to perceive the beauty in scripture. The first naiveté is to read only the words on the page. The second naiveté is to read with the eyes of the heart. On this deeper level, we experience the Sabbath not as a work of the law but as a work of beauty that invites us to transformation.

This second naiveté is the viewpoint from which we need to look at the diverse post-resurrection appearances in the Gospel. On the one hand, the Lord appears as a man like other men: he walks alongside the road to Emmaus with his disciples. For the first part of the journey, the apostles were on the level of the first naiveté, asking all the external questions about the interpretation of scripture and lost in their despondency. Symbols of bread and fish bring them to a deeper level where "he had been made known to them in the breaking of the bread" (Luke 24:35). The same theme occurs in the Thomas story. Moving out of the doubt that is in his head, he touches the wounds of Christ and says, "My Lord and my God!" (John 20:28).

At the Lake of Gennesaret, "just after daybreak, Jesus stood on the beach; but the disciples did not know that it was Jesus" (John 21:4). Only after the Lord had instructed them to rest once again does the beloved disciple recognize him: "That disciple whom Jesus loved said to Peter, 'It is the Lord!'" (John 21:7). It is, as it were, an inward recognition, which nevertheless remains shrouded in mystery. For after the catch of fish, when Jesus invites them to eat, there is still a strange quality about him. "Now none of the disciples dared to ask him, 'Who are you?' because they knew it was the Lord" (John 21:12). They knew from the eyes of the second naiveté, not from observing the Lord's outward appearance. The inner eye of love opened the heart to resurrected beauty.

In his apostolic exhortation *Verbum Domini*, Pope Emeritus Benedict XVI refers to the scriptures as a symphony. He uses the image of music, the harmony among notes as the hermeneutic, the way to encounter beauty in the word of God. He writes that "the tradition of Christian thought has developed the key element of the symphony of the word, as when St. Bonaventure, who in the great tradition of the Greek Fathers sees all the possibilities of creation present in the Logos, states that, 'Every creature is a Word of God since it proclaims God'" (§ 8). The Divine Artist speaks a creative word that brings energy into the universe. This word is not only meant to be read; it is also meant to be experienced in "what we have looked at and touched with our hands" (1 John 1:1).

The fathers of the Church used a beautiful phrase to capture this reality. They called it the *abbreviated word*. Jesus is the Word who became flesh. The God who created the heavens and earth came in this abbreviated form so that God could be heard, seen, and smelled. God has a face and can be touched and kissed. The Word was abbreviated so the human eye and heart could be expanded to embrace beauty beyond imagination. Heaven came to earth so that humankind could begin the journey to eternal beauty with the One who is beauty itself.

In this context, art, music, and poetry can be considered as abbreviated incarnations of the Eternal Word. Pope John Paul II wrote, "Art must make perceptible, and as far as possible attractive, the world of the spirit, of the invisible, of God. It must therefore translate into meaningful terms that which is in itself ineffable. Art has a unique capacity to take one or another facet of the message and translate it into colours, shapes and sounds which nourish the intuition of those who look or listen" (§12).

Christ used images in his preaching as a way of drawing people into the transcendent. We can be sure that as a good Jew, he prayed and sang the psalms. The psalms are filled with a wide range of images, feelings, and emotions. In the face of such beauty, what else could one do except sing? Pope John Paul II says, "The faith of countless believers has been nourished by melodies flowing from the hearts of other believers. In song, faith is experienced as vibrant joy, love, and confident expectation of the saving intervention of God" (§15).

The Second Vatican Council engaged the Church with the culture, especially the arts. Pope Paul VI, in a speech to artists on the steps of the Sistine Chapel, wrote: "The Church hopes for a renewed epiphany of beauty in our time and apt responses to the particular needs of the Christian community." We are invited to find God, not by withdrawing from the world, but rather by engaging with the world. This is the spirituality needed today. We are like the apostles on the road to Emmaus, recognizing Christ in the scriptures and the breaking of the bread. It is not enough to enjoy beauty. We need to follow beauty to that place where God lives. This is the mystical path that breaks down the barriers among religions, cultures, gender, and sexual orientation to see the God who beholds the beauty of all creation.

ARTISANS OF THE SPIRITUAL LIFE

Pope John XXIII opened a window at the Second Vatican Council. Pope John Paul II opened a door in the year 2000 to begin a century of jubilee. Windows and doors have opened up new spiritual worlds for the twenty-first century. In the pre-Christian tradition, and at various times even in the Christian tradition, there was a dualism that separated the world of matter from the world of the Spirit. The material world was perceived as inferior to the spiritual world and, thus, the concepts of beauty and spirituality were explicitly distinct from each other. The human body and the world were sinful entities that needed to be tamed. The spiritual life became a battlefield on which one fought with oneself to overcome our sinful nature. It was thought that only when we overcame our ugly, sinful nature could we move into the higher realms of the spirit. Holiness was an *otherworldly* state in which the body was repressed and the passions subdued and controlled.

We propose an alternative spirituality that celebrates the beauty of God's world. The locus of spirituality is a world in which theology, technology, and science harmoniously interact. Spirituality is not the passive experience of the Divine but rather our active reception of God's love. Mystics, artists, and poets are the ones who teach a spirituality of beauty. Artistic beauty comes from the deepest recesses of the human spirit. The artist is faithful to the tension of not knowing what the end result will be and allows the tension to lead him or her into the creation of art, poetry, literature, dance, and song.

The artist is the mystic who lives with the new tensions of the twenty-first century by listening more deeply. Like the prophet Elijah who flees into the hills, the artist does not find the Divine in the loud noises or the earthquake and thunder but in the tiny whispering sounds (1 Kgs 19:12). The artist listens with a third ear to the voices within the self, others, and God. The artist has what the Hebrew sages called *lebh shomea*, a listening heart.

The mystic-artist delves deeply into fearful places in order to discover beauty. Fear is often our first reaction to the unknown or what we perceive as different from ourselves. The mystic-artist does not fear but trusts the process of life. The artist is the mystic who unites religions and cultures to form a circle of beauty instead of walls of division.

The Canadian Jesuit philosopher Bernard Lonergan, in his book *Insight*, notes that finding meaning in life is the chief concern of most people.[3] Today, more than ever, there is a vast menu of choices for people attempting to find meaning in life. If one chooses the path of beauty, life itself can become a work of art and meaning will be found in the paints and colors of everyday life. Poets, artists, novelists, sculptors, composers, songwriters, filmmakers, photographers, and other artists have a particular responsibility in the world. They devote their full attention to creating works of beauty in the world. The eighteenth-century Scottish political philosopher Andrew Fletcher once said, "Let me write a nation's songs, and I care not who writes her laws," which tells us something about the importance of the artist in society. Art gets its power from the fact that its language is made up of symbols that have the ability to call up feelings. "It is not surprising," writes Albert Camus, "that artists and intellectuals should have been the first victims of modern tyrannies, whether of the right or the left. Tyrants know that there is in the work of art an emancipatory force."[4] Art calls the human person to deeper and higher levels. It challenges the shortsightedness of merely practical interests. The beauty of art is our only hope in a world that prefers the practical and productive to poetry.

THE STRUCTURE OF BEAUTY

The aesthetics of Hans Urs von Balthasar give a structure for a spirituality of beauty.[5] His theology is a kneeling theology. He gives theological legs to the poetry of Gerard Manley Hopkins, who wrote that "the world is charged with the grandeur of God."[6] Balthasar believed that there is an unbreakable bond between God and the world. The world is the place where God meets the human person and the human person encounters the Divine. Balthasar decried that we have lost sight of the attribute of beauty in the description of God as the One—good, true, and beautiful. His goal was to restore beauty to spirituality.

Balthasar considered the world to be the form that God uses for self-revelation and the place where we are invited into the beauty of God's presence. He joined faith and aesthetics as the way of touching the human person from head to heart, teaching that faith is the prerequisite for seeing the form of God's revelation accurately, and also the act whereby the event itself can be seen correctly. The beginning of beauty is God's revelation in the scripture that is the world. Balthasar's aesthetics were formulated on the absolute gratuity of grace. All of theology is a search for beauty and its written word attempts to capture the experience of beauty. Balthasar equates faith with an aesthetic recognition that would find God by listening to what God has created.

The Council fathers shared this viewpoint in the *Constitution on the Church in the Modern World*, stating that "literature and the arts are also, in their own way, of great importance to the life of the Church" and asserting that these art forms are uniquely capable of illustrating and clarifying aspects of the human condition in a way that "the knowledge of God is better manifested and the preaching of the Gospel becomes clearer to human intelligence and shows itself to elevate man's actual conditions of life" (§62). Beauty anchors the human person in the transcendent in an evolving world and shifting cultures. The Council recognized this when it asserted, "The Church acknowledges also new forms of art, which are adapted to our age and are in keeping with the characteristics of various nations and regions" (§62).

The goal of the framework of Balthasar and the Council fathers was to use art as the springboard for our journey back to God from the world. The traditional paradigm for the mystical journey is the doctrine of the three ways: purgative, illuminative, and unitive. The purgative way is the choice to turn away from sin and believe the good news. This puts one on the long and arduous path of illumination, the gradual reception of the light that comes from living a life of virtue. The final goal of the journey is unity with the source of our being, the center of all beauty.

In Balthasar's construct, the three ways are dynamic and cyclic rather than static and hierarchal. I would adapt his interpretation of the doctrine of the three ways to further create a template for developing and receiving beauty. In this framework, the pain of the suffering of purgation is to remove oneself from the culture in order to restore it to beauty. One is illuminated through beauty, which becomes the gateway for the light. Unity with the Divine is found in solidarity with the beauty created by our fellow artists and craftsmen.

St. Basil writes about the dynamic of beauty and divine grace in his *Homily on Psalm 29*, "…for I was beautiful according to nature, but weak, because I was dead to sin through the treachery of the serpent….Every soul is beautiful, which is considered by the standard of its own virtue." In the eyes of the Divine Craftsman, beauty in the human person is never lost; it is merely hidden because of the poor choices that we make. The journey from purgation to solidarity is a journey from beauty to beauty. Through sin, our beauty is hidden but, through grace, it is gradually revealed and restored. The structure of the journey to beauty is one that is sacramental because God is the beginning, middle, and end of the journey.

FINDING YOUR NAME IN GRACE

We were created by and for the One who is "ever ancient, ever new."[7] St. Augustine wrote, "Our hearts are restless until they rest in God."[8] Sixteen hundred years ago, the restlessness of Christians drove them into the desert of Egypt. There they wrestled with the basic restiveness of human nature. When they were at work, they felt drawn to prayer; when they prayed, they felt drawn to work; when they settled in one monastery, they became convinced that true spirituality could be found only in another monastery down the road. Because this restlessness struck hardest in the middle of the day, it became known as the *noonday demon*.

The challenge was to stay with the tension and wrestle with the restlessness.

Art, music, and literature can heal and rejuvenate us as we wrestle with the demons in the noonday sun. Beauty grounds us in those places where the demon of deception has divided us. The Hebrew word *Satan* is used for those things that divide and separate us from beauty. It is beauty that calls us back to our core identity. Like Jacob, who wrestled with the angel, we find out who we are by embracing our restlessness. We discover our name in the heart of God and the unique dimension of beauty that is reflected in the name God has given us. In his poem "The Naming of Cats," T. S. Eliot used the image of cats to describe the calming of restlessness that arises from discovering who and whose we are. As Eliot whimsically describes the three types of names a cat requires (the family name, the more dignified formal name, and finally, the cat's own true name), the pace of the words changes from agitated and jumpy to calm and sure. With simple words, the poet is able to convey the beauty that comes from having confidence in discovering the name God has given to you.

The name that God gave each of us is beautiful, but the ego renamed us long ago. To struggle with the noonday demons is to struggle with the ego. If you allow beauty to win the struggle, she will tell you who you really are in the mind and heart of God. The passion that emerges in the struggle will bring to the surface all of our desires, both good and bad. What moves you? What do you desire? Once you discover your true name, making decisions will come naturally. You choose those things that are true to your name. We are works of art, sacraments of God's beauty. As with Eliot's poem, a joyous and beautiful sacramental ceremony is far more beautiful than any description of its historical basis because it permits the beauty of the sacramental experience to transform and enliven the human spirit. Our God-given name, discovered in grace, is our sacramental gift of beauty to the world.

Pope John Paul II prayed in his *Letter to Artists*, "Artists of the world, may your many different paths all lead to that infinite Ocean of beauty where wonder becomes awe, exhilaration, unspeakable joy. May you be guided and inspired by the mystery of the Risen Christ" (§16). He will reveal your name to you. Like Eliot's cats, contemplation will open us to the Eternal One in whose love we rest.

ART AND CONTEMPLATION

Prayer is art; art is prayer. Both are creative expressions that fulfill the impulse to communicate. Art and prayer are expressions of creativity that are demonstrated in joyful praise and humble supplication. Both lift up the mind and heart to God. The communication between the artist and the viewer occurs with God as the meeting place for both. God is the One who makes this marriage happen.

Art and prayer have been intertwined from the very beginning: the first images painted on the caves were perhaps a plea before the hunt or a gratitude for the fruits of a good hunt. Art is a way of praying that embraces all of God's creation. It is no accident that the singing of birds, the smell of flowers, and the colors of the rainbow touch the human soul. We were made by God for beauty. You might even say that we are hardwired to appreciate beauty. Beauty is practical. It is concrete and calls one to attention. As the character Shug says in Alice Walker's novel *The Color Purple*, "I think it pisses God off if you walk by the color purple in a field somewhere and don't notice it."[9] God gives us beauty to teach us how to pray. The Lord used images in his preaching as a mirror to be held up before us. Images summon the entire range of feelings in the human heart. Art teaches us to respect all feelings and to stay with the feelings that ultimately become the raw material for the art of our prayer.

Art is a way of expressing faith. An excellent illustration of this can be seen in Rembrandt's *Self-Portrait as the Apostle Paul.* Look at the painting long enough and get into the artist's prayer, his reflection on St. Paul's teachings on faith and the sufficiency of grace. Grace is central to the writings of St. Paul. The *Diary of a Country Priest* captures this in the classic line, "All is grace."[10] Rembrandt expresses a visual link to grace through his use of light in highlighting the tip of his nose in the painting. The fruit of Rembrandt's prayer is his identification with St. Paul. The tone of the piece would suggest that Rembrandt is in prison with or in place of St. Paul. It is the interplay between darkness and light that demonstrates his theology of grace. It is light that opens up the darkness of the space. In doing this, Rembrandt is bringing his experience of God into the painting. It becomes for the viewer a glimpse into Rembrandt's heart and his true name. The viewer is invited into the experience but not expected to stop there. The painting becomes a springboard for the viewer to go deeper into the heart of God.

The genius of the artist is that he finds his name in grace by allowing St. Paul to lead him deeper into himself. The tension between light and darkness in the painting reflects St. Paul's struggle, "I do not understand my own actions. For I do not do what I want, but I do the very thing I hate" (Rom 7:15). St. Paul later speaks of "a thorn…in the flesh" and he begs God to take away the tension and darkness (2 Cor 12:7–8). What he is left with is, "My grace is sufficient for you, for power is made perfect in weakness" (2 Cor 12:9). Rembrandt shares with us the fruit of his contemplative prayer and reflection. He was receptive to God's grace during his struggles. Nothing changes and everything changes. All is grace; it is God's gift of beauty that empowers us to live with the tension of the struggle between light and darkness.

A similar theme is developed in Rembrandt's *Prodigal Son*. Rembrandt is both the older son and the younger son in the painting, the true self struggling with the false self. The darkness that he illustrates in his *Self-Portrait* is seen in the dark corner of the *Prodigal Son* piece, where the older son is depicted. Here we see the shadows into which human resentment can lead us. The movement into the light comes with the younger son. There is a transformation that takes place in the struggle, and the true self emerges in the younger son at the hands of a God who is father and mother to him.

The primary effect of the piece is to teach us how to contemplate God's beauty. Prayer is the tool that brings us through our human condition of sin back to the healing presence of God. Prayer does not make art by changing circumstances but by changing perspectives. The change is in how the younger son sees God. The two hands of the painting are different, one is masculine and the other is feminine. The younger son discovers the true self in a God who is so beautiful that no words can describe. God is the Prodigal One in his gift of grace that lifts our minds and hearts to the ecstasy of beauty.

BEAUTY CHANGES THE WORLD

Jesus came to show us the way to the Father and how to live in this world. He used metaphors in speech and actions to transform hearts of stone into hearts of flesh. He called people out of the familiar text of their religion into the text of life, inviting them to taste, feel, and touch. Jesus, as artist, taught us to see visually and intellectually.

Psychologists opine that the mind tires more quickly of hearing than of seeing, and that students retain from education 50 percent more of what is seen than heard. Carl Jung concluded that, in human life, representations rather than concepts make impressions more lasting and forceful. When the sculptor or artist brings color, lines, and texture, then theology becomes real life. Faith is no longer a definition of a belief to be defended but rather becomes the inspiration for works of beauty. Beauty has the power to change the fragmented society we inhabit. We live in a Babel of antagonistic tribes, tribes that speak only the languages of race, class, rights, and ideologies. Beauty transforms by speaking the language of love and unity.

The role of beauty in our lives is to help us find reconciliation and redemption in the midst of the world. As Christians, we live within our culture, and we neither baptize nor withdraw from it. The artist reaches into the culture to see in it the light of the Gospel. Christ established contact with the humanity of the publicans, tax collectors, and prostitutes he encountered in order to invite them into the beauty of salvation. Following his example, true artists depict the human condition in its fullness in order to lead viewers to salvation. The artist must be confident enough in his or her faith to be able to explore what it means to be human. At the heart of Christian humanism is the challenge to reach a new synthesis between the condition of the world around us and the unique ways in which grace can speak to the condition.

In his famous *Poplar Series* of paintings, Monet painted twenty-four pictures of the same row of poplars throughout the year, rushing to finish the series before the trees were cut down.

Striving to capture the light at a precise and different moment in each painting, he sometimes had only a few minutes to complete a painting before the light changed. Viewing the scene through the eyes of the artist, the beauty of the sunlight falling on the ever-changing pattern of leaves reminds us that God's beauty is infinite. Similarly, looking at the intricate beauty of the tree branches captured by the photographer Ansel Adams in his *Oak Tree, Sunrise* is to be transformed by the beauty of God's creation, all the more visible when stripped of color in the black and white photograph.

The incarnation challenges us to live with both the Divine and the human within ourselves. The artistic social stance in the world is precisely that, embracing the human with our eyes fixed on the Divine. We need creative imagination to do this. Imagination is the contemplative stance toward life that leads us to the love of all that is good, true, and beautiful.

Cairo is one of the most densely populated places that I have ever experienced. Mokattam is one of the poorest parts of the city, where there are thousands of rubbish collectors. They collect garbage throughout the day and bring it back to Mokattam, where they sort through it to see if there is anything they can salvage. The city is a dirty, smelly, depressing place. There is nothing of beauty to be found there. However, there are mountains overlooking the city. There is an artist who has devoted years to covering the cliffs with images of Christ in glory. People in the city can look beyond the garbage and see the transfigured Christ beautifully depicted before their eyes. The images proclaim that the people of Mokattam, poor though they are, are not garbage, but rather are God's children, created in the image of God. They are not only citizens of Mokattam; they are citizens of the kingdom, destined for glory. Indeed, this simple illustration is a magnificent expression of how beauty transforms our vision of the world without words and gives hope for the ultimate social transformation promised by One who is the Alpha and the Omega, the Beginning and the End, of all that is good, true, and beautiful.

CONTINUING ON THE ROAD TO BEAUTY

1. There are multiple definitions and understandings of the words *spirituality* and *beauty*. People mean many different things by these two words. What are your thoughts about these two words? How do you define *spirituality*? What does *beauty* mean to you? It would be worthwhile to read Pope John Paul II's *Letter to Artists*. His reflections on beauty and spirituality will help frame the discussion and refine your thinking on the relationship between beauty and spirituality.

2. Pope Emeritus Benedict XVI is a lover of the arts. Watch and listen to his reflections on beauty in *Art and Prayer*. He said that visiting churches, art galleries, and museums "is not only an occasion for cultural enrichment" but can also be "a moment of grace, an encouragement to strengthen our relationship and dialogue with God." He suggested that the beauty we find in these places can lead us to deeper levels of contemplation. Make a pilgrimage to a church, art gallery, or museum that is new for you. Notice something that draws your attention. Stay with it for as long as you can. Conclude this contemplative time with a prayer of praise and thanks for this work of beauty to the God who is the source of all beauty.

3. Engage the scriptures as an invitation to God's beauty through the written word. Pray with John 21:4–14. Read the passage aloud and then sit in silence for ten minutes to absorb the word. Allow images to come to mind as they emerge. Read the passage again and conclude with a few minutes in prayer of thanksgiving.

4. Read and savor Gerard Manley Hopkins' poem, "God's Grandeur."

5. Read T. S. Eliot's poem "The Naming of Cats." Follow the example of the cat and spend some time contemplating God's name for you.

6. View Rembrandt's *Self-Portrait as the Apostle Paul*. Notice Rembrandt's use of darkness and light as a technique for capturing the experience of grace in St. Paul's life and his own life. Does this painting change the way you think about St. Paul? How does it speak to you about your experience of God's grace in your life?

CHAPTER TWO

THE BEAUTY OF THE PRESENT MOMENT

One of the greatest challenges in our fast-moving culture is to live in the moment. In fact, I would go so far as to say that it is almost impossible. We try to cram as much as possible into each new twenty-four hours to accommodate overloaded schedules. We often find ourselves planning for the next moment or the next day rather than embracing the present moment.

The image of Jesus on the cross with two thieves on either side is a symbol of what it means to live in the present moment. The thief on one side was the thief of yesterday; the thief on the other side the thief of tomorrow. God is eternal and transcends time. The beauty of God is not confined to the past. God is not defined in the scriptures as "I was who I was." The past is over; we need to give up the hope of a better past and, rather, move on to live in the present. Nor is God defined as "I will be who I will be." The beauty of God is not limited to the future. When we find ourselves living in the future, we are being driven by our desire to control. God will take care of the future when it comes; it is not ours to control.

The God of revelation is defined as "I AM WHO I AM" (Exod 3:14). God is the God of the present moment. The essence of a spirituality of beauty is to choose to embrace each moment. Consider the beauty that occurs in nature. The spectacular beauty of a sunset or a rainbow is transient and can be experienced only for a fleeting moment. Let your thoughts distract you and you'll miss it. Instead, imagine yourself placing a picture frame around the moment. This is what artists, poets, and writers do. They frame the moment and allow God's beauty to pour over the canvas of life. All that we need and all that we could ever desire can be found in the present moment. Happiness, peace of mind, and healing are all in the moment when we are invited into the heart of God.

It is an interesting phenomenon that, despite the material success of our society, many people are not happy. In fact, psychological studies indicate that ours is a mildly depressed culture. Why is this the case? This happens because we choose to live life in the fast lane rather than choosing the path that Jesus teaches in the beatitudes. The fast lane in today's culture is often a bridge to nowhere. On that path, beauty is defined by external fashions rather than eternal truths. A focus on beauty as distorted to comply with the latest trends, rather than on the vision of the New Testament, plays to a narcissism in us that is anything but beautiful.

Thomas Friedman reflects on this phenomenon in his book *The Lexus and the Olive Tree*. He asserts that the world as we know it is about ten years old. As a result of the monumental advances in technology that have propelled the emergence of globalization, our world has been turned upside down. Friedman uses the image of the sumo wrestler for the world during the Cold War period. The two super powers, the United States of America and the Soviet Union, pushed against each other like two sumo wrestlers in a match at which the rest of the world functioned mostly as a spectator. With the collapse of the Berlin Wall in 1989, the world entered the next phase of its evolutionary development. The image of two sumo wrestlers was replaced by an image of multiple participants in the hundred-meter dash. The power base has expanded because now everyone has access to the same information. New venues for communication have revolutionized our world. There is no rest, for the race begins anew each day. It means little if you were yesterday's winner because today's race is a new one. The tempo of the hundred-meter dash is filled with frenzy and tension for it is driven by competition. The essence of competition is to move forward by stepping over another. God does not live there. Friedman points out that, with the abundance of information bombarding us in today's world, it is inevitable that many of the unimportant details will be forgotten. Among all the noise and information overload, there is only one thing that we must focus on. Friedman states, "If we forget whom we belong to, and if we forget there is a God, something profoundly human will be lost."[1]

"For what will it profit them to gain the whole world and forfeit their life?" (Mark 8:36). In the fast-paced world in which we live, it is easy to lose sight of what is important. When we choose to live in the valley of forgetfulness, the present moment has no value. Although the image of God is indelibly stamped upon us, our likeness to God is diminished when we forgo our humanity to focus on the race. Anthropologists believe that what distinguishes the human person from the animal kingdom in the Book of Genesis is the ability to choose to rest on the seventh day. For the remainder of the animal kingdom, there is no Sabbath. Every day is the same. When we choose to live this way, we choose to be less than human. We forget who we are and the reason for which we were created to live in this world.

In this way, Sabbath observance not only defines our humanity but also forms an alternative to the dominant culture. In the strict observance, the Jewish Sabbath begins on Friday evening. The wisdom of this conscious choice has deep psychological and physical truth. To use the analogy of a car, it takes the engine time to cool down after you turn off the ignition. It is next to impossible, if not impossible, to turn the switch off from the busyness of the workweek into the restfulness of the Sabbath. It is too much of a shock to the system, physically and spiritually, to do this. It is only after we have settled down on Friday evening that we are ready to begin the Sabbath on Saturday. The Sabbath is a time to be totally enveloped in the beauty of the moment. The alternative lifestyle of the Sabbath is one in which we pay attention, savoring every single moment. It is in the moment that the creative energies begin to flow. The Sabbath rejuvenates the artist within us.

The Jewish Sabbath is not meant to be an end in itself. It is a gateway to a new awareness of the power of beauty that will spill over into a new week. The new energy of the Sabbath is God-given. God is the creator of a Sabbath rhythm. This does not mean that we no longer work; it does mean that all of our works become expressions of beauty. In fact, beauty defines what it truly means to be human. The Sabbath brings us to beauty and makes us beautiful. It is the Sabbath that connects us with God, who has pitched a tent in the present moment.

It is for this reason that we are commanded, "Remember the Sabbath day, and keep it holy" (Exod 20:8). The Divine Craftsman models for us a way of life by working for six days and resting on the seventh. The Eastern Churches recognize the beauty that is inherent in following God's rhythm by choosing the word *dance* to describe what God does. They do not say that God *created* the world; instead they say that God *danced* in the world. If we allow God to lead the dance, we will then breeze through the universe with grace and joy. God's beauty is blowing in the wind; all we have to do is open up our sails. If we dance God's dance, we will enjoy the moment and be embraced by the warmth of the moment.

ART AS A PORTAL TO THE PRESENT MOMENT

God dances in the midst of the chaos of this world and creates beautiful things. The Book of Genesis describes a God who moves gracefully above the cosmos bringing symmetry and harmony. Scientists point out that movement is the first language that humans learn in the womb. In the first moments of life, we discover by sensing, feeling, touching, and moving. We can reach out to God and to other human beings because God gave us bodies. The actions of the human Christ embraced all that is human. "The Son of Man came eating and drinking, and they say, 'Look...a friend of tax collectors and sinners!'" (Matt 11:19). The Creator-God made us to be part of the larger universe, engaging our bodies and spirits with his and joining hands with one another to enjoy his creative energy in the present moment.

Living in the present moment is to dance in the universe, feeling the breeze of the wind, the warmth of the sun, and the gentleness of the night air. A friend of mine has a sign hanging from her doorknob reminding her, "Life is not about waiting for the storm to pass; it is about learning to dance in the rain." Beauty summons you to wake up, be alert, and to pay attention. The saints and the poets understand this. The Indian poet Kabir urges us, "Wake up!…go out and walk in the rain!"[2] and experience with zest and energy the world that we live in. Likewise, the poetry of Maya Angelou is filled with a passion for life and its beauty in all its forms. In her inspiring poem "On the Pulse of Morning," which she read at President Clinton's inauguration, Angelou writes about the gift of each new day and urges the reader to see each morning as a new beginning, facing an endless horizon.[3]

Poets intuit Jesus' promise, "I came that they may have life, and have it abundantly" (John 10:10). If you are asleep or not paying attention, life is something that will happen to you while you are busy doing something else. Our first impulse may be to avoid the silence and the empty spaces where hidden beauty is buried. Don't go with that impulse. St. Ignatius of Loyola wisely noted that often what is immediately satisfying is ultimately disappointing; and sometimes what is immediately disappointing can be ultimately satisfying. Reflection and openness to the beauty of each moment pave the way that leads to peace and to the fulfillment of our truest dreams.

In their book *The Addictive Organization,* Ann Wilson Schaef and Diane Fassel write that American culture has characteristics of the addictive personality.[4] They believe that we are collectively compulsive and in denial. Compulsivity and denial distract us from the present moment by pushing us into the past or the future. The basic flaw in this dynamic is that it diminishes contemplative living. If we are reflective, we will choose what we will do rather than being driven into frenzied activity. If we are aware, we will instinctively know that we can do nothing without God's help and the support of one another. The prayer that is said immediately following the Lord's Prayer in the liturgy asks for deliverance from our compulsions.

> Deliver us, Lord, we pray, from every evil,
> graciously grant peace in our days,
> that, by the help of your mercy,
> we may be always free from sin
> and safe from all distress,
> as we await the blessed hope
> and the coming of our Savior, Jesus Christ.[5]

The word *evil* is not used here in a strictly moral sense but rather connotes a broader description of harm. In the specific context of a spirituality of beauty, evil is to allow oneself to become distracted from the beauty of the present moment. A very wise person told me, "Scripture says that you should pray always, and if you do not pray always, you should at least pray sometimes." I asked him, "How do you do this?" He answered, "Each morning when I get up I spend some time praying." I asked, "How long do you pray?" He responded, "As long as it takes me to get focused." I then asked, "What about the rest of the day?" "Very simple," he said, "whenever I lose my focus because of my addiction to compulsivity and denial, I go back to the present moment to refocus on God's love."

Our culture is one in which we like to grab and hoard things. The grabbing is a distraction that removes us from the present moment. Grabbing taps into the dark hole of narcissism where we think the world revolves around our needs and wants; hoarding focuses our attention on the future. Coming back to the present moment invites us back into that space where God reigns and allows us to indulge in the fountain of God's beauty. If we live in the moment, we will find our hearts overflowing with gratitude. Living this way brings us to a place where, instead of grabbing and hoarding, we begin to cherish and to behold. All of life becomes a work of art. Eating an apple, for example, becomes a moment of awe for the gift of beauty that an apple is. Seen in this way, it not only will nourish the body but also will refresh the spirit.

Our *to do* lists cram our days and block out the power of the moments within those days. I have a friend who loves to make lists of things that he thinks he must do each day. He loves to check these things off at the end of the day. This gives him a sense of accomplishment and fulfillment. At the end of the day, when he reviews his daily routine, he will write down anything that he did during the day that he forgot to include in the morning. He does this for the pleasure that it gives him in checking another item from his list. His spiritual director suggested that he examine what he was doing and alter this practice. He invited him to bring his list to God each morning and to pray for the grace to truly live every single moment of the new day. If the list was very long, he told my friend to ask for the grace to do the first one very slowly so as to begin the day in peace and not in frenzy. He then told him to take a second look at the list and ask God to show him if there was anything on his list that was not of God. If so, he suggested that he pray for the grace not to do it. His spiritual director invited him to enjoy the *doing* and not just the *getting done*.

THE EYES OF FAITH

Jean-Pierre de Caussade, in his classic work *Abandonment to Divine Providence,* wrote, "Faith sees that Jesus Christ lives in everything and works through all history to the end of time. It is faith that interprets God for us.…To be satisfied with the present moment is to relish and adore the divine will moving through all we have to do."[6] It was de Caussade who coined the phrase *the sacrament of the present moment*. It is faith that awakens an alternative consciousness that views the world through new eyes. For example, a scientist could look at water and see H_2O. St. Francis of Assisi could look at the same water and see *Sister Water*. A group of people can be at the same event and have very different experiences. A bride and groom at a wedding are certainly having a very different experience from the janitor who is standing in the back of the church waiting for the ceremony to be over so he or she can clean up. One person walks down a busy city street and sees dirt and hears noise. Another person walks down the same street and sees a smile on someone's face and hears birds chirping in the air. Faith opens the eyes to the present moment and prepares the heart to go to deeper places.

Mary models for us what it means to embrace the moment with the eyes of faith. We sing the hymn *Stabat Mater*. Mary stood beneath the cross. She was steadfast in her commitment to stay present in the moment. While she stood at the foot of the cross, she looked up and saw something that gave her the courage to stay there while everyone else fled. She did not resist the experience of the moment, which led her to feel the pain of the crucified Christ and to see a new kind of beauty revealed in the pain. Faith holds life in the balance and gives us the courage to stay in the space where life is happening.

In their paintings, Dürer, Titian, and El Greco all depict Mary as the one at the center on Pentecost receiving the Holy Spirit. Mary, who remained faithful to the pain at the foot of the cross, is filled with joy as she experiences the fruits of the resurrection. The present moment becomes sacred space where the living God dwells; we come to love the present moment through faith. The two enemies of faith are fear and caution. Fear blocks us from life and cripples us from going where the spirit wants to bring us.

Henry Ossawa Tanner powerfully captures these dynamics in his magnificent painting, *The Annunciation*. He depicts Mary as a young Middle Eastern woman. She is sitting on the side of her bed wringing her hands, overcome with fear and bewilderment. She is torn between the darkness of fear and the light of trust. A bed that is unmade and a rug that is ruffled depict the ordinariness of her life. Tanner is known for his use of light to convey religious concepts. Instead of the usual portrayal of the archangel Gabriel in the painting, Tanner uses light as a powerful expression of religious experience. His painting shows the light, indicating the presence of the angel Gabriel, jumping into the darkness of Mary's fear. She is not a passive spectator in this piece. She actively stays in the moment, feels the fear, and makes the choice of saying, "yes" to the light. Mary receives the light; she is "full of grace." The representation of Gabriel by a shaft of light reminds us of the beauty of God's presence in this moment, which would otherwise have been an unimaginably dark time for Mary. The act of faith represented in the painting is to not be overcome by fear but to move into the glorious light.

The moment of trust behind Mary's beautiful act of faith was captured by Robert Morneau in his poem "Fiat," which he wrote upon viewing Tanner's *Annunciation*. He described Mary's look of fear and worry as she studied the shaft of light in her room and then the moment of grace that changed the world: "Somehow she murmured a 'yes' / and with that the light's love and life / pierced her heart / and lodged in her womb." Mary is our model in faith because she is the one who said "yes" to light, then received the light, and brought the light of Christ into the darkness of the world.

Caution is the second enemy that kills the light of faith. St. Luke, in chapter 1 of his Gospel, draws the contrast between Zechariah and Mary. Like Mary, Zechariah's initial reaction to the message of the angel was fear. It is remarkable that although he was part of the privileged class as a man and priest in first-century Judaism, Zechariah was not able to say "yes" to the present moment and receive the light. Instead, he was immobilized by doubt and indecision. Frozen by his inability to take the risk, he saw only the dark side and missed the pull of God's grace into the healing power of the moment. To be overly cautious is to choose to be paralyzed by the darkness and miss the beauty to which God invites us each day.

It was pure naked faith and not intellectual speculation that freed Mary to say "yes" to the light. Beauty happens in a fraction of a second in the present moment. We must be alert and ready always to *carpe diem*, to seize the moment, and more importantly to allow ourselves to be seized by the moment. We need to be careful not to get lost in endless debates and doubts. Sometimes the way is not clear and a process of discernment and consideration is needed to make a thoughtful decision about the choices to be made. The choices will become clear when we get in touch with the deepest desires of the human spirit. This will give an indication of what God's will is for us. The basic question during any discernment process is, "What is best going to keep me in a relationship with God?" When we live in our heads and revisit the same points over and over again, it is no longer about doing the will of God but rather obsessing about fears and anxieties. Faith is not about obsessive thinking and calculation; it is about living, living in the here and now of God's presence. Jean-Pierre de Caussade gave good advice when he wrote, "You have only one duty: to keep your gaze fixed on the Master, listening intently to what he wishes and then do it at once....To live by faith is to live joyfully."[7]

CHOOSING HAPPINESS IN THE PRESENT MOMENT

God does not want us to be miserable. God's desire or will for us is happiness. The choice is ours each day: choose life or choose death. I keep a sign on my bathroom mirror that reads, "You are now looking at the person who is responsible for your happiness today." You might think, "What if things are going badly in my life? What if bad things happen to me? How is it possible to be happy?" I would respond, "Why would you want to add misery or unhappiness to your list of troubles?" Happiness is not a feeling; it is a state of mind. Take the example of the optimist and the pessimist. One wakes up in the morning and says, "Good morning, God," while the other says, "Good God, morning." As they both walk outside to begin the day, they see a bed of newly blossomed flowers. One says, "Look, how beautiful these flowers are!" The other responds, "Yes, they are beautiful, but there must be a grave underneath them."

The famous "Serenity Prayer" by Reinhold Niebuhr is rooted in the reality of God.[8] He proposes a way that will bring us happiness in the present moment. I share his prayer together with my comments about his words:

- *"God grant me the serenity to accept the things I cannot change, the courage to change the things that I can, and the wisdom to know the difference."* We are invited to accept the rhythm of daily life as it unfolds. The underlying truth is that there is a plan that is bigger than us in the ebb and flow of life. We accept what we cannot change and choose to focus on the things that we can change. When we live in this way, we carry the peace we have found in the present moment to the world around us.

- *"Living one day at a time, enjoying one moment at a time."* All we have is the twenty-four hours that God gives us for today. Think of life in this way, twenty-four hour segments. What we can do is live fully for today. When we find ourselves not living to the fullest, just start the day over again.

- *"Accepting that hardships are the way to peace."* We do not choose hardships; hardships choose us. We will find happiness if we embrace hardships instead of resisting these intrusions into our daily existence. We can learn a great lesson from the birds of the air. Each year around the feast of St. Joseph on March 19, the swallows leave Capistrano and begin the journey north. Several years ago, people noticed that, as the birds were leaving, they placed twigs in their beaks. It appeared that the birds were foolishly choosing to carry hardships with them. However, the seemingly stupid birds would drop the twigs on the ocean when they got tired, then would float, using the twigs to rest until they could continue the journey. The very thing that appeared to make the journey more difficult was, in fact, what made the journey possible. What appears to be a burden can become a blessing. The only way to discover this truth is to stay with the burden of the cross and to be transformed by it in the present moment.

- *"Accept the sinful world as Jesus did, as it is and not as you would like it to be."* In the present moment, we actively receive the world as it is rather than just passively resigning ourselves to whatever happens to us. Our salvation and happiness are in the present moment. If we do not find it there, we will not find it anywhere.

- *"Trusting that you will make all things right if we but surrender to your will so that I might be reasonably happy in this world and eternally happy in the world to come."* God will make all things right. St. Augustine wrote, "God writes straight with crooked lines." Our happiness depends on whether we really believe this. As the poster says, "God does not do windows." Windows are our attitudes. St. Paul writes, "Let the same mind be in you that was in Christ Jesus" (Phil 2:5). Christ the teacher models for us that our peace lies in our ability to surrender to the will of the Father in the moment.

Niebuhr's prayer is a roadmap for healthy and happy living. His way of life captures the dance of the Sabbath rhythm for which God created us.

DISCOVERING THE TRUE SELF IN THE PRESENT MOMENT

The chief struggle for every human being is the battle between the false self and the true self. The ego is the false self, the mask that you wear in the world. The false self is trying to be something other than that for which you were created. We are led around by the ego. The ego brings us everywhere except to the present moment. The ego fears the present moment for it has no power in the moment. The ego is exposed for what it really is.

One of the great mysteries in life is that only we humans try to be something other than what we are. Imagine for a moment that an elephant decided that it wanted be a bird or a bird decided it wanted to be a cow. Original sin is the fundamental flaw in human beings. It is the refusal to be our true selves as sons and daughters of God. The false self brings nothing but unhappiness and frustration into our lives. The present moment calls us back to fidelity, to the true self that is made in the image and likeness of God.

The battlefield becomes an altar when we place the ego on it, letting it go so that it is no longer controlling the direction of our lives. When we do this, we no longer serve the ego; the ego is now serving us. This lifelong process is incorporated into the *paschal mystery*. This phrase simply means that, through baptism, Christians enter into the journey of reclaiming the true self by incorporating into their lives the dying and rising of the Lord Jesus. At the broadest level, the paschal mystery encompasses the entire life of Christ, his birth, life, death, resurrection, and ascension. These events cannot be separated into different categories. It is the entire Christ-event that brings about salvation. The word *paschal* embodies this reality. The use of this word helps us avoid focusing only on the cross or only on the resurrection. Both realities are equally included in the word *paschal*, which comes from the Hebrew *Pesach* and refers to the Passover, Israel's deliverance from the Egyptians when the angel of death passed over the doorposts marked by the lamb's blood. The spring rituals of the surrounding cultures influenced the form of this annual remembrance of Passover. For the Jews, however, it is much more than a celebration of the freshness of springtime. It is a festival of redemption. At the annual Passover meal, the Jews remember their deliverance from slavery to the Egyptians. In doing so, they are, not only remembering a past event, but also celebrating that Yahweh is still with them and will walk with them into the future. Each Jew is challenged to internalize this event into his or her own life. In other words, the gift of freedom was given to the Jewish people collectively, but each Jew has also been given that gift in his or her personal life experience.

The Christian version of this is the invitation to enter into the mystery of Christ's death and resurrection. This transformation of becoming like Christ is a mystery because we often do not even realize that this is what is occurring moment to moment in our daily lives. It is essential to understand that paschal mystery spirituality has more to do with taking on Christ's attitude than mimicking his actions. St. Paul, in his Letter to the Philippians, expressed it well, "Let the same mind be in you that was in Christ Jesus, who, though he was in the form of God, did not regard equality with God as something to be exploited, but emptied himself, taking the form of a slave….He humbled himself and became obedient to the point of death—even death on a cross" (Phil 2:5–8).

Each Christian is invited to take on the attitude that Christ had toward life. The Holy Spirit moves individual Christians to do this in ways that will vary from person to person. Christians who take their call seriously must listen carefully in the present moment and discern where the true self emerges and becomes a reality in the world. The paschal mystery in our lives has much to do with rediscovery in our time of the humanity of Christ. The implications of this for living out the paschal mystery are very important. The fact that Christ was fully human means that he lived out his human existence exactly as we do; he was not just playacting. He lived out the paschal mystery in the everyday ordinariness of his human existence, as well as in his sacrifice on the cross.[9]

Bodily death is the bridge that leads to eternal life. St. Francis of Assisi courageously and joyfully greeted death with the beautiful salutation, "Welcome, my Sister Death."[10] Where did he get the courage and strength to do this? Without a doubt, it came from his belief and love for the Christ who died and rose again. The Eucharistic celebration gave St. Francis, as it gives us, a faith vision to live life, every single minute of it, and at the same time to welcome Sister Death: "For as often as you eat this bread and drink this cup, you proclaim the Lord's death until he comes" (1 Cor 11:26). The little deaths of daily life are sacraments that prepare us to embrace the final death that brings us back home.

Kabir expresses a similar sentiment in his poem "The Time Before Death," urging his readers to focus on the Divine as they live their lives on earth in order to be prepared for life in the hereafter.[11] The whole point is to *die* daily so that our final death will bring the full blossoming of the true self. Death is our sister that brings us to new and deeper places both now and in eternity. When should we start this spiritual practice? St. Paul tells us, "Now is the acceptable time" (2 Cor 6:2).

The true self emerges over a lifetime, and it is in eternal life that the true self fully emerges in glory. St. Catherine of Siena wrote, "All the way to heaven is heaven."[12] If we peek into heaven, we get a tiny glimpse of who we really are. The invitation is to begin to make heaven happen now by embracing the moment. The false self refuses to live in the present moment. When we die to the false self, we can then say together with St. Paul, "It is no longer I who live, but it is Christ who lives in me" (Gal 2:20).[13]

THE BEAUTY OF THE PRESENT MOMENT AS SPIRITUAL PRACTICE

There are many excellent works that explain practices and methods for living in the present moment. Although some of these are very helpful, I would like to propose an alternative approach. Let works of beauty bring you to the celebration of the present moment. Works of beauty can cultivate a mindfulness that brings us out of our heads into the wonder of the present moment. Works of beauty take us from a prosaic *doing* mode to a poetic *being* mode.

Mindfulness teaches us how to be nonjudgmental and to accept the mystery of the moment. It is a way of paying attention that wakes us from our sleep. De Caussade writes that a focus on God's will elevates our spiritual lives to the point that they become the center of our existence. He expresses the importance of the present moment in this way, "We must be active in all that the present moment demands of us, but in everything else remain passive and abandoned and to do nothing but peacefully await the promptings of God....The way to pure faith is simple: it enables us to find God at every moment."[14] Works of beauty are ways in which de Caussade's vision of "soaring like eagles"[15] carries us into the winds of love. He also urges us to accept life's humiliations as ways that we empty ourselves in the face of beauty so that the "hole in the soul" can be filled with the ecstasy to which the master artist invites us. Let us explore some spiritual practices that open us to the infinite possibilities of transformation through beauty.

Art opens the spirit through seeing, hearing, and touching. Art forms are an absolute affirmation of the power of the incarnation that moves one from linear thinking and toward unitive thinking. The artist takes the raw materials of the world—color, sound, wood, and stone—and transforms the ordinary into powerful expressions of the spirit. This transformation happens through the imagination that taps into the very creativity of God. Samuel Taylor Coleridge wrote that the poet brings his or her whole soul into the activity. Coleridge attributed the beauty of poetry to the gift of imagination, which he saw as the human faculty that creates beauty. Coleridge referred to the imagination as "…that synthetic and magical power, which reveals itself in the balance or reconciliation of opposite or discordant tendencies.…[It] dissolves, diffuses, dissipates, in order to recreate."[16] In this view, the magical power of the imagination is always active, working to unify and idealize the creative process. Beauty is the outcome, when the writer brings fresh enthusiasm and profound feeling anew to old and familiar objects.

Creative language guides us toward beauty in a different way. The instruments of literature are words that move hearts to cultivate the beauty of the moment. Literary art forms have the potential to weave words into a tapestry of beauty. In the poem *Ash-Wednesday*, T. S. Eliot highlights the power of words with the concept of "the Word within." It is the contact with the Word that gives spirit and life to the word spoken or written. The written word that comes from the Word can be redemptive and transformative. The word that is inspired by the Word of Gospels can move us into new space and openness toward our fellows. The wonderful scene from Shakespeare's *King Lear,* inspired by the beauty of language, brings us to new and deeper levels of compassion:

> Poor naked wretches, wheresoe'er you are,
> That bide the pelting of this pitiless storm,
> How shall your homeless heads and unfed sides,
> Your loop's and window'd raggedness, defend you
> From seasons such as these? O, I have ta'en

Too little care of this! Take physic pomp;
Expose thyself to feel what the wretches feel,
That Thou mayst shake the superflux to them
And show the heavens more just.[17]

Works of poetry such as these force you to slow down. You simply can't race through a poem. It needs to be sipped slowly like a cup of espresso. The poet looks at small things in the world through a microscope and brings together diverse elements into a single piece. Dun Scotus called this the *scandal of the particular*. The concrete shocks, wakes us up, and calls us to attention. Nicholas of Cusa called poetry a bridging, a *coincidence of opposites* that perks the imagination and evokes wonder. Gerard Manley Hopkins demonstrates the beauty of a coincidence of opposites in his poem "Pied Beauty," proclaiming, "Glory be to God for dappled things," which initially captures the attention simply by providing such an unusual object for gratitude that the reader does a double-take. Describing the juxtaposition of colors and patterns found in nature, Hopkins creates verbal images with a stream of hyphenated and *dappled* words. The creation of these mind-pictures forces the reader to slow down and produces a sense of gratitude for the beauty that the poet is describing. This magnificent piece touches the heart, mind, and imagination. It resonates with our experience and it brings us into that contemplative space where all things are possible.

Dance is a medium often overlooked as a tool that is included in our spiritual practices. Dance enhances music through bodily movements that truly make the Word take flesh. The Hebrew Scriptures use the image of David dancing before the ark to the tune of multiple instruments, a freeing expression of art that uses the whole body. To become involved in the movement of dance is the most concrete and immediate way of getting out of one's head into the present moment.

In fact, movement is our first language. We move in the womb and we move when we first come into the world. Movement long precedes the spoken word as a medium of self-expression in the human journey. Dance is the universal language that captures the rhythms and cycles of nature and transcends all cultures, races, and creeds. Dance defies Jansenism that would deny the human body. Dance uses the beauty of the body and its movement to live in the moment and to glorify the Creator.

Rublev's icon of the Trinity demonstrates the movement of dance within the godhead in its graceful rhythm of the three. The heads of the three men are inclined toward one another, their hands gesturing relationship through movement. The dance of God is expressed in Hippolytus's Easter hymn: "O thou leader of the mystic round-dance! O thou leader of the spiritual marriage feast!"[18] The Logos is the leader of the dance, which moves within the world. Its very movement invites us to join in the dance.

Icons open a unique window into the beauty of the present moment. St. Paul writes, "He is the image *(eikon)* of the invisible God, the firstborn of all creation" (Col 1:15). Just as Christ is the image of the Father, the icon is an image that invites us into the mystery of God. Although the history and theology of icons is a fascinating one, let's focus on the magnetism of icons to lift up the heart to the heights of contemplation. In fact, as you look long enough at an icon, you begin to notice that the icon is looking at you. This interplay between knower and known, between seer and seen, promotes an active connection between the person and the icon that pulls the art into the domain inhabited by the viewer and, thus, focuses attention on the present moment.

The nativity is one of the favorite subjects of icons. The spirituality of the nativity icons is expressed in the prayer of the Christmas vespers, "What shall we offer you, O Christ, who for our sake has appeared on earth as man? Every creature made by you offers you thanks. The angels offer you a hymn; the shepherds their wonder; the earth its cave; the wilderness the anger; and we offer you a virgin mother."

There is a rich fifteenth-century icon of the nativity from the Novgorod school that captures the spirit of this prayer. In the icon, the whole created world gathers around Christ, who is in the center, in order to give praise. Even the animals join in the chorus. The nativity does not take place in an idyllic stable but rather alongside a rugged mountain. The figure of Mary, the *Theotokos* (God-bearer), is prominent. She is the finest thanksgiving to God. Joseph is depicted in the lower left-hand corner, looking somewhat perplexed in the midst of this extraordinary event. We are invited by the angels to join in the chorus of praise and adoration as we are moved by this icon, which looks at us and invites us into the present moment.

Finally, there is music, a popular and powerful venue that pulls us into the moment with gusto. Music moves us out of ourselves into another reality. Think of music without words that invites you to listen even more deeply, to attune the ear to the sound of the incarnation, to hear what others cannot hear, to go to that place where you can see with your own eyes and touch with your own hands. Watch a small child dance to a song on her mother's iPod and you will understand that the delight in music is innate and does not require language. The beauty of the repetition in the chanted Litany of the Saints is a powerful stimulus for contemplation that flows from the sounds, rather than from the words themselves. The intricate melody of a Mozart concerto has the power to engage one person's spirit in a way that is not dissimilar from that prompted in another by the harmonies of ragtime jazz music or in another by the guitar riff from Led Zeppelin's "Stairway to Heaven."

Music is the universal language. My mother, who was an immigrant from Italy, learned English by singing songs. Once again, we see that beauty is sometimes counterintuitive. It begins with the heart and only then travels to the head.

> ...I heard the voice of many angels surrounding the throne and the living creatures and the elders; they numbered myriads of myriads and thousands of thousands, singing with full voice,
>
> "Worthy is the Lamb that was slaughtered
> to receive power and wealth and wisdom and might
> and honor and glory and blessing!" (Rev 5:11–12)

Music, painting, literature, dance—all of these expressions of art invite us to linger in the present moment, to appreciate the beauty of the work, and to connect with the wonder of our world as seen through the eyes of the artist. These and other media of artistic expression pull us into the beauty of the moment. Works of beauty give us glimpses into the Divine that transform the moment into treasured graces. For this reason, de Caussade was absolutely correct when he referred to the present moment as a sacrament. In James Joyce's *A Portrait of the Artist as a Young Man*, Stephen and his friend Lynch examine the nature of true art as an experience of the Divine and come to a wonderful conclusion that encapsulates the beauty of the present moment. "The instant wherein that supreme quality of beauty...is apprehended luminously by the mind which has been arrested by its wholeness and fascinated by its harmony is the luminous silent stasis of esthetic pleasure, a spiritual state very like…the enchantment of the heart."[19]

The present moment is the sacrament where we encounter the God who touches us with the light and warmth of a burning ember. This is indeed the enchantment of the heart.

CONTINUING ON THE ROAD TO BEAUTY

1. The prophet Isaiah wrote, "If you call the sabbath a delight…then you shall take delight in the Lord, and I will make you ride upon the heights of the earth" (Isa 58:13–14). Are you too busy to take a Sabbath weekend? Remember that the Chinese pictograph for *busy* is composed of two characters: *heart* and *killing*. Delight in the Sabbath! Begin on Friday evening and conclude on Sunday evening. Relax, enjoy, and pray. Structure the weekend in any way you like. The one absolute rule is: NO Work. After the weekend, try to live the week ahead with a Sabbath rhythm. Work hard but make time for play and prayer. Get a friend or family member to share the Sabbath experience with you, so you can learn and reflect together.

2. View Henry Ossawa Tanner's *Annunciation*. Does this piece change the way you see Mary? If so, how? What is most striking to you about the piece—the rug, the bed, or the water jug? What is Mary doing with her hands? Where is the angel Gabriel? Does this piece deepen or change your understanding of religious experience?

3. Michel Quoist wrote, "We are not God. We are simply the image of God and our task is gradually to discover that image and set it free." Sit in a comfortable chair, feet flat on the floor, hands folded, and eyes closed. Just remain this way for twenty minutes and experience God's image in you.

4. Take a virtual tour of the Convent of San Marco in Florence. Fra Angelico lived there and painted his famous frescoes on the wall of the monastery. Pope John Paul II declared Fra Angelico the Patron of Artists. Tour the monastery, enjoy the frescoes, and live in the moment.

5. Make a virtual visit to Saint Rocco's Square in Barcelona to enjoy the wonderful *Ode to Joy* and practice the sacrament of the present moment.

6. Experience the beauty of your world through one of your senses (sight, sound, touch, or smell). Sit in the backyard or take a walk in a park and make a mental list of everything that you experience through that one sense. Give thanks for the sounds of the birds, the coolness of the grass, or the tiny flowers growing between the rocks. You can do this for a week and share with a friend, focusing on a different sense each day.

CHAPTER THREE

BEAUTY AND
FORGIVENESS

Often what prevents us from seeing beauty in the outside world is the fact that we fail to see beauty in ourselves and other people. Forgiveness is the key that can unlock this door for us. God has forgiven us and we would be wise to do the same. The God who forgives invites us to share that gift with others whom we have excluded from our lives due to past hurts. The God whom we meet in the present moment is the One who unconditionally loves and forgives us. This same God invites us to offer the gift of forgiveness to those whom we do not see as beautiful.

Before we can create beauty and see beauty in the world, we must first see beauty in ourselves. The God who loves us unconditionally sees beauty in all creation. The prayer "Known," written by Charles K. Robinson, is a meditation on how it is God's love and presence in our lives that makes us beautiful:

> I know you. I created you. I am creating you. I have loved you from your mother's womb. You have fled—as you know—from my love. But I love you nevertheless and not-the-less and, however far you flee, it is I who sustain your very power of fleeing, and I will never finally let you go. I accept you as you are. You are forgiven. I know all your sufferings. I have always known them. Far beyond your understanding, when you suffer, I suffer. I also know all of the little tricks by which you try to hide the ugliness you have made of your life from yourself and others. But you are beautiful. You are beautiful more deeply within than you can see. You are beautiful because you yourself, in the unique one that only you are, reflect already something of the beauty of my holiness in a way which shall never end. You are beautiful also because I, and I alone, see the beauty you shall become. Through the transforming power of my love you shall become perfectly beautiful. You shall become perfectly beautiful in a uniquely irreplaceable way, which neither you nor I will work out alone. For we shall work it out together.[1]

Beauty is like a covenant between God and us. God offers and we receive. When we believe that we really are beautiful, then we can focus our eyes to see beauty in those who trouble us or hurt us. Without beauty, there can be no forgiveness and with beauty, all things are possible, even forgiving our enemies.

Rev. Julie Nicholson, an Anglican priest, took a sabbatical from her pastorate because she felt that she could no longer preach forgiveness and reconciliation following the murder of her daughter in London's July 7, 2006, bombings. She had to deal with the ugliness of her pain and anger before she could continue as an instrument of God's beauty. "Easter," she says, "is supposed be the final proof that love is stronger than death. But how much comfort is that for parents who have to stand, like me, at the foot of the cross?" Rev. Nicholson realized that she had to go through a healing and forgiveness process because her pain had blinded her. The gospel message is essentially about forgiveness. Not to deal with forgiveness is not to deal with the Gospel of Jesus Christ. Nicholson says, "It is not something I can put down like a shopping bag. What do we really mean by faith and forgiveness? I think that the world should be challenged to consider this, as I have been."[2]

Another powerful story about forgiveness is Maya Angelou's experience of being raped at the age of seven, as told by Sr. Camille D'Arienzo. "So brutal was the violation that she was hospitalized. From her bed of pain and shame she spoke her rapist's name. Arrested and released, he was later found kicked to death. Because she had uttered his name, the child blamed herself for her abuser's death…[Eventually], she embraced this formula for self-healing: one who has suffered a great evil must name it, learn from it, forgive it, and move forward with courage to focus on the future. Forgiveness had no power to change her past, but it had enormous power to mold her future."[3]

Forgiveness restored beauty to the lives of Julie Nicholson and Maya Angelou. Bill Moyers later described what happened to these two women. "Victims of evil must cope with the ugly graffiti that is scribbled on the walls of their psyche. Can they forgive the evildoers? Should they?" An answer can be found in the wisdom of the Quakers, who remind us, "Forgiveness is a gift that we give ourselves."[4]

FORGIVENESS: WHAT IT IS NOT

Before we can understand that forgiveness is a pathway to beauty, we must first understand what forgiveness is not. Forgiveness is a mystery that we cannot control or fully comprehend. It is God's grace that makes forgiveness happen. The psychological and emotional healing that follows the miracle of forgiveness cannot be predicted nor can it be measured.

The old axiom "Forgive and forget" is not good advice. Forgiveness is not forgetting; would that it were so easy! Superficial forgiveness can do more harm than good and deprives one of the opportunities to learn from mistakes and injuries. For example, nothing is learned if holocaust survivors do not tell their story. The story is retold so the same evil will not happen again. Our minds and hearts can become dulled to the effects of evil. When we choose to remember, forgiveness becomes possible. It takes a strong sense of self to acknowledge hurt and it takes humility to verbalize the depth of our hurt.

Instead of forgetting the past, redemptive remembering is looking at the past with the power of the risen Christ, who heals what happened *then* in the power of the *now*. Christians draw on this power to forgive themselves and their enemies. Although reconciliation is not a guaranteed outcome of the process, it is at least possible. One would need a good reason not to seek reconciliation. For example, there is little you can do if the other does not want reconciliation. Conversion cannot be one-sided. If the other were unwilling to change damaging behaviors, it would be foolish to engage in a reconciliation process.

A spiritual *one-upmanship* can deceive us into thinking that forgiveness happens instantaneously without a healing process. To paraphrase the German Lutheran theologian Dietrich Bonhoeffer, this is what I would call *cheap forgiveness*. It is neither long lasting nor deep rooted because it is not grounded in reality. *Costly forgiveness* is to do what Jesus did in offering forgiveness and, then, going through the painful process of getting there.

The path toward forgiveness is one that must include acknowledging the hurt of our anger. Repression of anger can lead to passive aggressive behaviors. Anger and hurt are natural reactions when we are offended. We need to confront these issues if we are to reach a deep and lasting forgiveness. It is not helpful or healthy to pretend that nothing has happened and that nothing has gone wrong when we are hurt by another. Denial not only shuts the door to the possibility of forgiveness but also opens the door to further emotional and spiritual damage. We know from the Gospels that there are times when Jesus got angry. For example, he threw the moneychangers out of the temple, chastising them for making his Father's house a den of thieves (Mark 11:17). On another occasion he expressed his anger toward Peter when he said, "Get behind me, Satan!" (Mark 8:33).

Possibly, the most difficult thing to understand is that forgiveness is not simply a brutal act of will. A white-knuckle approach will not yield the desired gospel outcome. Although we believe in the gospel ideal, it is not easy to deal with hurt feelings from broken relationships. Christians are held to the highest standard of forgiveness. No other religion requires that its followers turn the other cheek (Matt 5:39) and forgive their brothers and sisters "not seven times, but, I tell you, seventy-seven times" (Matt

18:22). What is most unique about Christian forgiveness is that Jesus teaches us that the other should be forgiven even if he does not deserve to be forgiven. He pushes this to the limit and teaches that we should forgive even if the other does not ask to be forgiven (Luke 6:37–38). These are standards that are impossible to attain except through the grace of God, because "for God all things are possible" (Matt 19:26).

Forgiveness does not absolve the offender. Only God gives absolution. What we can do is open the doors of our hearts when we are ready. Both parties in a hurtful relationship are in need of the healing that God offers. We open ourselves up to the other, and together we open ourselves up to the God who wants to enter into the process of restoring what has been broken. However, forgiveness and reconciliation are not two sides of the same coin. Forgiveness does not necessarily include reconciliation, but reconciliation necessarily includes forgiveness.

Self-sacrifice is noble but it is not the essential ingredient for the miracle of forgiveness to occur. In many ways, we could say that forgiveness is a form of self-interest. When we do not forgive, there is a lack of wholeness in our lives. There is a hole in the soul that cannot be filled. It is as if we are going through life carrying an extra piece of luggage under our arms. Our resentments are toxic. They damage the human spirit. Bitterness casts out love and this deeply scars the human heart.

Jesus teaches us in the Gospel of Matthew that if we are bringing our gifts to the altar and remember that we are not at peace with another, we should "leave your gift there before the altar and go; first be reconciled to your brother or sister, and then come and offer your gift" (Matt 5:24). This is a profound psychological and spiritual truth. We cannot be at peace with God unless we are at peace with one another. It is impossible to pray to God unless we can talk to other people.

Forgiving trespasses is a lifetime's work. In interpreting the Hebrew Scriptures, the Jewish rabbis make a significant distinction when referring to peace and forgiveness. The Hebrew phrase *lech l'shalom* ("go *to* peace") was used when Jethro said farewell to Moses (Exod 4:18). He was sending him forth to begin a process that would ultimately lead to peace by liberating the Israelites from Egypt. In contrast, the phrase *lech b'shalom* ("go *in* peace") is reserved for the deceased, because the completeness that comes with peace can only be attained in death. This is the blessing that David gave to Absalom on their last encounter before Absalom's death (2 Sam 15:9). It is only in life that we work *toward* peace. With this in mind, forgiveness might be seen as a way of going toward peace as opposed to continuing cycles of hurt and revenge. It is the never-ending process that is completed only in the New Jerusalem.

There can be no peace without justice. Forgiveness does not absolve the administration of justice. For example, Pope John Paul II forgave his attacker's actions, but the man continued to serve a prison sentence. For the Christian, it is love and not hatred for the other that motivates the desire for justice. It is not wishing punishment for the sake of punishment. Instead, it recognizes that the offender needs to be restrained so he or she will not cause further harm to self or others.

The cycle of life is filled with the pain of shattered relationships. We are never finished with the work of forgiveness. We always need to go deeper in working through our hurts. Enjoy any reprieve before new hurtful situations happen in your life. It is not in completing the task that we find beauty. We find it in our openness to new levels of inner beauty that comes from working through our anger, frustrations, and hurts. These are new opportunities that God gives us to begin the difficult path of letting go, so that we can find the new surprises that the beauty of God's love offers us.

WHAT IS FORGIVENESS?

In many ways, forgiveness defies definition. It means different things to different people. The beauty of forgiveness is like a diamond's multifaceted sparkle. Religious, academic, and political leaders have wrestled with the meaning of forgiveness over the centuries, and the literature on forgiveness covers a wide spectrum. For the Christian, it is simple. Forgiveness is what disciples of Jesus do because he told us to do it.

There is no Christianity without community. Therefore, anything that disrupts or destroys the community must be confronted so that we can begin to restore what is so sacred to us. The underlying spirituality is that the community is the face of God that reflects God's love to the world. The community as a whole is disrupted by fractured relationships among its members. The entire community has a stake in the forgiveness that its members offer to one another.

Forgiveness is the way that leads to inner freedom. It breaks the chains of the past and takes us out of bondage. The biblical image that I would use is that of Lazarus in the tomb. The Lord comes and says, "Unbind him, and let him go" (John 11:44). The failure to forgive places us in the stench of the tomb. Jesus desires to unbind us and make us free. At the Easter Vigil, the wounds of Christ are marked by the insertion of five grains of incense on the paschal candle. The priest then proclaims them to be "holy and glorious."[5] Forgiveness allows us to unite our wounds with those of Christ. We are free to allow our sufferings to be redemptive, "rejoicing in my sufferings for your sake, and in my flesh I am completing what is lacking in Christ's afflictions" (Col 1:24).

At the heart of forgiveness is the opportunity to acknowledge that what we observe in others is often a projection of our own shortcomings. Forgiveness begins with compassion for oneself. This is the most difficult thing for us to do. As we look at our sins and mistakes, we feel guilty and hopeless. These feelings never come from God. God invites us to open ourselves up to healing and forgiveness through gently examining and acknowledging our mistakes. Without this first step, the forgiveness of others is never possible.

St. Paul, in his Letter to the Romans, offers the clearest and most challenging message about forgiveness:

> Bless those who persecute you; bless and do not curse
> them. Rejoice with those who rejoice, weep with those
> who weep. Live in harmony with one another; do not
> be haughty, but associate with the lowly; do not claim
> to be wiser than you are. Do not repay anyone evil for
> evil, but take thought for what is noble in the sight of
> all. If it is possible, so far as it depends on you, live
> peaceably with all. Beloved, never avenge yourselves,
> but leave room for the wrath of God; for it is written,
> 'Vengeance is mine, I will repay, says the Lord.' No, 'if
> your enemies are hungry, feed them; if they are thirsty,
> give them something to drink….Do not be overcome
> by evil, but overcome evil with good. (Rom 12:14–21)

If we take St. Paul's words seriously, we will pray for those who hurt us and ask God to bless them. We ask for the grace to see them as God sees them. If you have trouble forgiving, think of Jesus on the cross. The human Jesus struggled to forgive. He prayed, "Father, forgive them; for they do not know what they are doing" (Luke 23:34). My speculation is that the human Christ found it hard to forgive and asked the Father to do for him what he himself could not do at that moment. To paraphrase the old axiom, "To err is human but to enter into the process of forgiveness is divine." Our human pain from life's hurts brings us to our knees as we pray, "Father, forgive them for they know not what they do. Help me eventually to do the same."

RESTORING BEAUTY
THROUGH FORGIVENESS

Forgiveness is the opposite of revenge. In contrast to revenge, forgiveness is an attitude that is willing to be open to new beginnings through inner healing. Revenge replays vicious cycles of old scripts. Forgiveness confronts us with another human being and challenges us to let go of the past and move into the future. The process of forgiveness demands that we renounce revenge. It requires us to let go of the desire to hurt the other in any way. We do not wish any other harm nor will we punish the other by emotionally withdrawing from them. We may choose to end a relationship. We do not do this out of anger but rather from the conviction that continuing the relationship will do further harm. Regardless of what we might choose to do about continuing a relationship, for our own well-being we need to let go of resentments. The word *resentment* comes from two Latin words: *re* and *sentire*, which means to think the same thing over and over again. It is the deadening *broken record* that allows another to rent space in your head. Before you know it, they have bought the house and resentment has taken over your life.

Forgiveness offers an alternative that moves beyond such generic categories as white/black, Israeli/Palestinian, and Protestant/ Catholic. Forgiveness is interpersonal because it puts a face on the other. The focus is not on the offense and more on the offender; it is less on the past and more on the future. Ultimately, forgiveness is an act of faith, "forgetting what lies behind and straining forward to what lies ahead, I press on towards the goal for the prize" (Phil 3:13–14). The prize is shalom, "that peace of God, which surpasses all understanding" (Phil 4:7).

Our fractured relationships are a microcosm of the wars, hatred, and divisions in the world. Social philosopher René Girard argues that the human tendency is to project all our frustration and anger on the other and believes that scapegoating is the cause of all wars and divisions.[6] Scapegoating divides, wounds, and destroys our world and can become a vicious cycle that is passed on from one generation to the next. Most troubling is that religions are often at the heart of conflict that destroys others. If we study the sacred texts of the world religions, however, we will discover that each one espouses forgiveness and love. In fact, it is the literalist or fundamentalist interpretation of religious texts that is often at the root of violence in our world. An arrogance can emerge from such an interpretation that would have us think that we are speaking *for* God rather than *to* God.

It is our Christian belief that only the cross can break the cycle of violence. "Father, forgive them; for they do not know what they are doing" (Luke 23:34) replaces the "eye for eye, tooth for tooth" (Exod 21:24) morality of the Hebrew Scriptures. Christ is the One who becomes sin on the cross so that it will no longer have any power over us. He takes on the sin of the world and does not return violence for violence. The cross is victory over sin and death that overcomes the ugliness of deceit and injustice and restores beauty through the victory of the resurrection. We join in the chorus of beauty when we follow the example of Jesus. Jesus did not return violence for violence. He turned the other cheek and, thereby, broke the cycle of scapegoating.

We join the chorus of beauty when we break the cycle of scapegoating by letting go of revenge and resentments. There are several things that one can do to enter into this process.

- *Begin by exploring the injury.* Be clear with yourself as to exactly what happened and why you are injured or alienated from the other.

- *Name the pain and feel it.* It is important to acknowledge that you are in pain; you "have a toothache." When you have a toothache, your whole body hurts.

- *Ask yourself: Why am I reacting this way?* What is the damage that has been done?

- *Make a choice as to what your next steps will be.* At least be willing to enter into the process of forgiveness, whether it takes weeks, months, or a lifetime. The choice is between the weeds and the wheat: to wallow in the weeds of resentment or to move forward toward the wheat of healing and forgiveness.

The decision to go down the path toward forgiveness carries with it a commitment to engage in what can be a challenging process. It is easier to talk about forgiveness than it is actually to forgive. To paraphrase Dostoyevsky, forgiveness in dreams is beautiful but in reality it is hard work.[7] Gospel forgiveness demands that we face anger, guilt, and resentment. Forgiveness leads us beyond the past into an unknown future where the fullness of beauty will be restored for all eternity.

THE TWELVE STEPS OF ALCOHOLICS ANONYMOUS

The twelve steps of Alcoholics Anonymous are a tried and tested way of restoring beauty into broken lives.[8] These steps are based on the scriptures and the Spiritual Exercises of St. Ignatius. The twelve steps lead to healing and forgiveness of life's hurts by tackling the core issues and opening the door to new freedoms. Steps four through ten focus on reconciliation and forgiveness. Let us look at these particular steps of a process that has the potential to restore beauty to our lives.

- *Step Four: Make a searching and fearless inventory.* It is frightening to remove our masks and see ourselves exactly as we are in the eyes of God. It is our fears that prevent us from doing this. Adam and Eve hid in the garden after they ate the forbidden fruit, imprisoned by their fear and shame. We, too, want to hide from our imperfections, but God calls us into the light to see ourselves as we are. There is no such thing as a perfect human being; we are all flawed. We need to own our feelings and take responsibility for our lives rather than blaming everyone else for the scars of life's hurts. We can become so self absorbed that we are numb to the ways we have hurt others. It is a grace-filled opportunity to be able to look at one's experience as a broken vessel on the rocky sea of life and to accept the hand of God that is pulling us out of the wreckage.

- *Step Five: Admit to God, to ourselves, and to another human being the exact nature of our wrongs.* St. Ignatius of Loyola warns against the false spirit who would convince us to keep things secret and hidden from trusted companions and those who can help us. They can bring objectivity when we are lost in the midst of desolation and confusion. When we find ourselves hiding, a maxim to recall is that "we are as sick as our secrets." The fact that we can begin to articulate to another what is going on inside ourselves is the beginning of the healing process. There are many ways we can do this. A few examples are the sacrament of reconciliation, psychological counseling, or a heart-to-heart conversation with a good friend or with a sponsor in a twelve-step program. When we begin to take these kinds of actions, we start to realize that not only do we need to forgive but we also need to be forgiven. What we do on the personal and interpersonal levels eventually needs to extend to national and global relationships that are broken by differences in religion, race, culture, gender, and sexual orientation.

- *Step Six: Be ready to have God remove these defects of character and ready to have him remove our shortcomings. Step Seven: Humbly ask God to remove our shortcomings.* All human beings at times act out of self-centeredness. This behavior is what St. Paul refers to when he writes, "I do not do what I want, but I do the very thing I hate" (Rom 7:15). As we get in touch with these basic flaws, the thorns in our sides, we begin to recognize that only a power greater than ourselves can restore us to sanity. In these steps, we ask God to do for us what we cannot do for ourselves.

- *Step Eight: Make a list of all persons we have harmed and make amends, except when to do so would injure them or others. Step Nine: Make direct amends to such people wherever possible, except when to do so would injure them or others.* The power of these steps is their clarity and simplicity. No words are minced. Once we start down this path toward healing, we are always invited to go one step further. Forgiveness and healing are no longer abstractions on this journey. We are now invited to embrace real people and events that have ruffled our feathers. To go to another and ask for forgiveness takes deep humility and to forgive another takes heroic courage.

- *Step Ten: Continue to take personal inventory and promptly admit when we are wrong.* Each day brings new opportunities and new obstacles. The work of healing is never completed. This step challenges us to deal with our transgressions as quickly as possible so that we do not become poisoned by our hurts and fears. At the end of each day, it is important to reflect back over the day, to recognize and acknowledge our mistakes, and to begin the process of healing.

The practice of these steps is not the only path that can be taken, but they do offer a way that can lead to a deep and abiding peace.

PRAYER, FORGIVENESS, AND HEALING

Forgiveness cannot happen without prayer. The prayer of the heart confronts us with the primacy of forgiveness. To put it in the simplest terms, prayer is a way of reaching God and of God reaching us. It is very much like that wonderful image in Michelangelo's fresco of creation, depicting the touch between the hand of God and the hand of Adam as God reaches out to create human life. In prayer, we are open to receiving the touch of God's hand, which is there already, just waiting for our hands to reach out. Prayer is simply a time of listening and loving. It is the meeting of the human self with the mystery of the Divine.

The lack of forgiveness in our lives prevents us from seeing the beauty of the God that fills every tiny space in this universe. Prayer opens up that window for us. St. Paul writes that we should "pray without ceasing" (1 Thess 5:17). Prayer is building an altar in the midst of violence and conflict in order to bring beauty back into our hearts.

Jesus teaches us to pray for our enemies, for those who persecute us. Prayer is the most powerful tool that we have as we meet enemies within ourselves and in our wider world. The fact that we think we have enemies indicates that there is something going on in our hearts that blocks beauty. When we pray for our enemies, we begin to recognize that it is often not the other who is hurting us, but rather our perceptions of self that we are projecting on the offender. When we pray for our enemies, we are also praying for ourselves. Prayer forces us to let go of the illusion that the other is different from us. God's vision for us is unity.

Forgiveness offers wings to prayer. Prayer has the capacity to free us from our illusions. We reach this point by listening to the voice of the Spirit who leads us to the heart, which is the seat of our emotions. The Lord tells us, "Whenever you pray, go into your room and shut the door" (Matt 6:6). That is another way of saying: go into your heart, to that place where you can be totally yourself, and take off the mask. When you go into the room of your heart, you take everyone with you, especially those with whom you are not at peace at the moment. Going into the room of your heart and closing the door is to make room for God and the other through solitude. When you pray, you rise from your knees touched by grace even if you do not feel it. We express this belief in the Common Preface IV when we pray, "For, although you have no need of our praise, yet our thanksgiving is itself your gift, since our praises add nothing to your greatness but profit us for salvation."[9]

We are challenged each day to metanoia. It is here that we come to our senses, come back to our true selves. This is not an introspection, a turning in on oneself, but rather a reflection, an entering into oneself. Forgiveness, where we begin to let go of judgments, laying aside the sword and removing our protective walls, is prayer's ally. It is here that we acknowledge our need for spiritual renewal through God's grace. The German theologian Karl Rahner suggests that we experience the spirit of God most deeply through performing the ordinary tasks in everyday life with anonymous decency, when our good deeds are not seen or appreciated by others. In his *Reflections on the Experience of Grace*, Rahner challenges us to value the times when we sacrificed or forgave someone and received no recognition or reward, "…for the experience here is the experience of eternity."[10] When we pray, the Spirit leads us to the experience of beauty. The miracle is forgiveness.

FORGIVENESS IN POETRY AND ART

The themes in poetry and art are frequently about healing and forgiveness. Each time we experience these treasures in poetry or art, another layer of insight and healing is uncovered. Beauty brings us to those places where forgiveness and healing occur in the deepest way. Let's look at a piece of poetry and a piece of art that offer this possibility for us.

St. Francis of Assisi expressed his spirituality of forgiveness as one that opened his mind and heart through poetry and song. His "Canticle of the Creatures" is an uplifting piece of Italian poetry that St. Francis and the brothers sang throughout the streets of Assisi, calling people to praise and forgiveness.[11] St. Francis composed the beautiful piece after he had received the stigmata in September 1224. After receiving the stigmata, he returned to the leper colony to be with the least brethren, the Christ who lives among the poor. This was followed by a very hard winter during which his vision worsened. He was almost totally blind and his eyes were covered during the day because the light of the sun was too painful. In the midst of terrible pain, he composed the words of the canticle and wrote the melody. He told the friars to sing it with him and to go through the streets of Assisi, dancing with this song on their lips.

In his poetry, Francis invited all creation to join him in praising God, rejoicing in the beauty of the sun and the moon, the wonder of the wind, water, and fire, and the beautiful flowers that God has created. The sun, moon, and wind became symbols of the Trinity for him. He saw the God who is Father, Son, and Spirit reflected in the universe, and this is why the world is a beautiful place even in the midst of pain and suffering. Importantly, in this same poem, St. Francis declares that forgiveness and acceptance of life's burdens are equally worthy of our gratitude and praise:

"Praised be You, my Lord, through those who give pardon for / your love and bear infirmity and tribulation. / Blessed are those who endure in peace / for by You, Most High, they shall be crowned." The song ends with an appreciation of the gift of achieving bodily death while in a state of grace: "Blessed are those, whom death will find in Your most holy will, / for the second death shall do them no harm."[12]

The heart of the canticle is about forgiveness. The bishop and mayor of Assisi were battling with each other and saw each other as enemies. St. Francis included the line about forgiveness to the canticle to use his poetry to end the feud that was tearing the city apart. In addition, he sang his canticle to help him deal with the feuds going on in his own life. He was having trouble forgiving the hurts inflicted by his father, Pietro Bernadone, and by his Father in heaven for creating an imperfect world that he experienced in his personal sickness, the decadence of the Church, and the divisions within the community that he founded.

The final line of the poetic piece was intended to be sung after every verse, "Praise and bless my Lord and give him thanks and serve Him with great humility." St. Francis understood that it was only humility that would enable him to seek forgiveness from others and to give forgiveness to others. When he experienced this miracle, he went to eternal peace with the parting words, "Let us begin, brothers, for up to now we have done nothing."

Forgiveness is also a frequent theme in art. Let us look at a simple image that teaches the meaning of forgiveness. The image of the Peruvian saint Martin de Porres, reprinted here from a popular holy card (artist unknown), became a symbol in the seventeenth century of reconciliation among the races and the conflicts of the animal kingdom. St. Martin de Porres was a mulatto, the illegitimate son of a Spanish nobleman and an African slave, who

St. Martin de Porres

became known for his humility and compassion for all living things. We see in him the prophecy of Isaiah fulfilled: "The wolf shall live with the lamb, the leopard shall lie down with the kid, the calf and the lion and the fatling together, and a little child shall lead them" (Isa 11:6). St. Martin becomes the little child in this piece who teaches us how to reconcile conflicts.

The picture depicts an episode in the kitchen of St. Martin's Dominican convent, where St. Martin often fed stray animals in between caring for the poor and the sick. The story behind this picture was told by Fray Fernando Aragones and referenced during the beatification of St. Martin. So great was St. Martin's compassion and ability to engender peace that "at the feet of the mulatto St. Martin, a dog, a cat, and a mouse were eating from the same bowl of soup, natural enemies eating peacefully side by side!"[13] The wider context was an oppressed culture into which Martin did not fit as an illegitimate child of mixed race. To add to his isolation from the culture, some think that he had Moorish, that is, Islamic, leanings within his Christian world. This piece of art is one example among thousands that depicts the reconciliation among cultures, races, and religions.

The joy and peace that come from forgiveness sustain a reservoir of love in our hearts and enable us to perceive God in the people around us. As we go through the strengthening and healing process of discernment, forgiveness, and reconciliation, we find ourselves surrounded by the beauty of God's love and grace. The warmth of God's eternal love inspires us to see the beauty in ourselves and in other people, preparing us for the eternal beauty that comes in the warm embrace of a loving and forgiving God.

CONTINUING ON THE ROAD TO BEAUTY

1. Place yourself in God's presence and receive God's love, mercy, and compassion. Bring to the surface a past hurt that has been somewhat healed. Think of ways in which the hurt has made you a more loving and compassion-

ate human being. How have you grown from the hurt? Thank God for the new life that you have as a result of growing from this hurt and ask the Lord to deepen the healing that he has already begun in you. Conclude by reading John 20:19–23. Imagine Jesus wishing you "Shalom" (Hebrew for *to fix what is broken*) and pray that you can be an instrument of God's *shalom* for those whom you will meet today.

2. View Rembrandt's *Prodigal Son*. What do you notice about the Father's hands? What do you notice about the older son? What about the younger son with the shaved head and the broken sandal? Let the portrait speak to your heart and conclude by reading Luke 15.

3. The *Kiss-Dismiss* Exercise: Think of a person who has troubled you and has rented space in your head. In your imagination, kiss, bless, and pray for the person. And then dismiss the person from your mind. Try this exercise for several days and think about adapting this as a regular spiritual practice.

4. Step four in the twelve steps of Alcoholics Anonymous is "Make a searching and fearless inventory of ourselves." Step five is "Admit to God, to ourselves, and to another human being the exact nature of our wrongs." It is not an easy task to write down the areas in your life that are in need of healing and then to share this with another person. Think about doing these two steps. It is a major investment of time and energy that will make a big difference in your life.

5. Pray St. Francis of Assisi's "Canticle of the Creatures."
   Pay particular attention to the lines, "Be praised my
   Lord, through those who forgive for love of you," and,
   "Happy are those who endure in peace." Take these two
   lines and use them as a mantra for several days, allowing
   the words to go from your lips, to your head, then to
   your heart.

CHAPTER FOUR

BEAUTY AND
GRATITUDE

Works of beauty open our hearts to gratitude. At the same time, gratitude opens our eyes to see beauty. St. Bonaventure and St. Ignatius of Loyola both taught that ingratitude was at the root of all sin. St. Bonaventure believed that sin is the crime of ingratitude. St. Ignatius wrote, "Ingratitude is the most abominable of sins...for it is a forgetting of the graces, benefits, and blessings received. As such it is the cause, beginning, and origin of all sins and misfortunes."[1] An ungrateful attitude blinds us to beauty and often brings dissonance and darkness. Gratitude is the antidote to the effects of darkness in our world. Meister Eckhart said it well when he wrote that if "thank you" were the only prayer we ever said, it would be enough. It is a spirituality of gratitude that restores harmony and gives hope.

Cardinal Suenens was once asked, "Why are you a person of hope, even in these days?" His answer provides a framework for a spirituality of gratitude and hope: "Because I believe that God is new every morning. I believe that God is creating the world today, at this very moment. He did not create in the long ago and then forget about it. That means we have to expect the unexpected as the normal way God's providence is at work."[2] Suenens's faith freed him to cross the bridge from gratitude to hope.

Gratitude is an attitude to be cultivated that comes from deep within the human soul. It is a good thing to be thankful and to develop the habit of saying, "Thank you." In fact, the annual North American Thanksgiving holiday is a wonderful event in the calendar year. Gratitude, however, is more than an acknowledgment for good things. Gratitude invites thanks even when things are not going well or during times of uncertainty. The reason is that gratitude is an expression of faith and not a mere *thank you* for a good deed done for you. Gratitude flows from the experience of love and expresses itself in joy. G. K. Chesterton wrote that from gratitude come "the most purely joyful moments that have been known to man."[3] Suenens clearly expressed what he believed to be the source of hope and gratitude when he said, "I am hopeful because I believe that the Holy Spirit is still the creating Spirit, and that he will give us every morning fresh freedom, joy, and a new provision of hope, if we open our soul to him."[4] Living by the Spirit is a way of life that elicits our attention and demands a response.

To be absorbed in gratitude is a gift of the Spirit that makes us channels of hope for others. Hope is not a dream, but a way of making dreams become reality. "Happy those who dream dreams and are ready to pay the price to make them come true!"[5]

Gratitude and hope are two sides of the same coin. A spirituality of gratitude is especially needed in these difficult times where there is a deficit of hope. Gratitude calls forth the best in us because it leads us to the source of the world's beauty. Hope stems from our images and beliefs about God, which are expressed in a spirituality of gratitude.

IMAGES OF GOD

Language cannot express the fullness of the mystery of God. The Hebrew Scriptures tell Israel's story of its experience of God. The multiple and sometimes contradictory images of God in the scriptures challenge us to be open to images that defy definition. We find some of these images in the prophetic books of the Hebrew Scriptures, especially Hosea, Jeremiah, and Isaiah. The images found in these books have inspired artists throughout the centuries.

The God of Hosea is a parent-God who loves the child unconditionally and is heartbroken when this child runs away. Although the child deserves punishment, the loving parent extends mercy and kindness. "When Israel was a child, I loved him....It was I who taught Ephraim to walk....How can I give you up, Ephraim?...My compassion grows warm and tender" (Hos 11:1–8). This theme is a pivotal one that became part of Israel's consciousness based on the experience of God's unending faithfulness and patience as Israel wandered and strayed from its covenant with God.

Jeremiah continues the parental tradition of God images. His images arise from his experience of love. He writes, "Is Ephraim my dear son? Is he the child I delight in? As often as I speak against him, I still remember him. Therefore I am deeply moved for him; I will surely have mercy on him, says the Lord" (Jer 31:20). Isaiah uses images that capture the feminine and maternal dimension of God. He writes of the parent-God, "Can a woman forget her nursing child, or show no compassion for the child of her womb? Even these may forget, yet I will not forget you" (Isa 49:15).

God is the One who relentlessly pursues us. He is the persistent One, the hound of heaven. Jeremiah writes, "I am going to bring them from the land of the north, and gather them from the farthest parts of the earth, among them the blind and the lame, those with child and those in labor….I will lead them back, I will let them walk by brooks of water, in a straight path in which they shall not stumble" (Jer 31:8–9). God is the One who is leading us on the journey toward a glorious homecoming. "I will lead the blind by a road they do not know….I will turn the darkness before them into light, the rough places into level ground" (Isa 42:16). Isaiah's experience of God was one of mercy and kindness. It prepared his heart to receive beauty and to write beautiful words about the God whom he experienced.

The many images of God in the scriptures testify that the human quest for knowing God will never be fully satisfied in this life. The God of mystery is indeed a God of surprises. The Book of Jonah depicts the human struggle in accepting God's desire for us. The prophet Jonah did not want to go to Nineveh to condemn its wickedness. When Jonah attempted to end his life on the ocean, God sent a whale to rescue him. He lived in the belly of the whale for three days. When he reached shore, he preached his sermon of repentance to the Ninevites. The God that he imagined to be angry was filled with mercy and compassion for these people. Jonah was the angry one because he could not accept a God who would forgive the Ninevites while the Israelites were still suffering.

The Book of Jonah demonstrates how we project our anger on God and recreate him in our image and likeness.

God images develop and change in the scriptures. These images are influenced and limited by the dominant culture at the time. For example, in the sixth century BC, when the prophet Jeremiah lived, farming and pottery making were common occupations in Jerusalem and surrounding areas. The prophet used these experiences as metaphors to describe images of God. Jeremiah uses this image in his text, "Can I not do with you, O house of Israel, just as this potter has done? says the Lord. Just like the clay in the potter's hand, so are you in my hand" (Jer 18:6). As the human person is formed in the potter's hands, images of God are refined: "So I went down to the potter's house, and there he was working at his wheel. The vessel he was making of clay was spoiled in the potter's hand, and he reworked it into another vessel, as seemed good to him" (Jer 18:3–4).

In addition to the ones already noted, there are many other images of God in the scriptures. For example, some of the images in the Hebrew Scriptures depict Yahweh as a farmer (Isa 5:1–7; 1 Kgs 4:25; Jer 13:12–14); Yahweh as midwife (Job 38:28–29; Isa 66:9; Ezek 16:2–5); God as disciplining father (Prov 24:32; Prov 13:24); wisdom as a woman (Prov 8:17; Sir 14:22–27) who serves a meal (Prov 9:1–6).

The New Testament frequently uses stories to express the ways in which the life of Jesus changed people's experiences of God. For example, in the story of the adulterous woman (John 8:5), Jesus is inviting the people to move beyond the Law of Moses (Lev 20:10; Deut 22:20) that would require vengeful punishment. St. Paul is the best example of one whose images of God changed dramatically once he knew Jesus. In the Acts of the Apostles, Paul is filled with anger and violence toward the followers of Jesus. In the conversion story, Jesus does not condemn Paul but instead loves him and invites him to conversion (Acts 9:1–22). Paul describes the exuberant feelings about his new experience of God: "…nor anything else in all creation, will be able to separate us from the love of God in Christ Jesus our Lord" (Rom 8:39).

Many of us grew up with an image of God based on St. Anselm's theology of *atonement,* which holds that the Father sent Jesus to the world in human form because actual humans were incapable of obeying and pleasing God to the extent of which God was worthy.[6] St. Anselm's theology held that Jesus had to die on the cross to make reparation to the Father for the sin of humankind. This was the predominant image taught in the Baltimore Catechism. Duns Scotus and the Franciscan school held an image of God that was diametrically opposed to St. Anselm's teaching. The Franciscan view holds that God did not send Jesus into the world because of our sin. Rather, Jesus came as a sign and symbol of God's great love for us in order to invite us into the circle of love that is the Trinity.

William Holman Hunt's famous painting *The Light of the World* depicts a God image closer to the Franciscan School than to Anselmian theology. His image is a very challenging one because he places the onus on us. He illustrates this by depicting Jesus knocking on a door that has no handle and, thus, cannot be opened from the outside. The painting conveys the message that Jesus knocks on the door, but the door can only be opened from within. It is up to us to open the door and invite Jesus into our hearts; the initiative is ours. On viewing this piece, C. S. Lewis wrote, "…the doors of hell are locked on the *inside.*"[7] Although the incarnation is God's invitation to intimacy with himself, it is up to us to respond to the invitation.

The Holy Saturday descent into hell that is at the core of Balthasar's teaching on beauty presents a compelling God image. Jesus rescues Adam and Eve from the darkness of hell and carries them into the light of the resurrection. Overwhelmed by God's redemptive love, Balthasar writes, "The love of God is great beyond comparison. It has no ground except itself and always comes from farther away and leads still farther on than I could have thought and imagined....What I thus bring about has already long ago been brought about by the love of God."[8]

Art and poetry expose us to images of the God who invites us into his loving heart. Once we are transformed by his passionate love, we are challenged to live loving lives, to become works of beauty. Balthasar believed that gratitude was the best response to God for the gift of his love: "It would be ungrateful to the redeemer and giver of grace if one would not see in grace something wholly new."[9] In reflecting on the incarnation, he wrote, "It is not our movement toward God, but God's movement to us. It is heaven interrupting our world...the descent of the divine light among human beings not only to shine on, to illuminate, to purify and to warm them, but, through grace, to make them also shine with a light not of this world."[10] Praise flowing from our lips is the surest sign that we are in touch with the God whom St. John defines as love.

PRAISE AND GRATITUDE

The psalms are the most beautiful expressions of praise and gratitude in the entire Bible. Psalm 136 is a stunning example of the beauty of gratitude. The psalm begins, "O give thanks to the Lord, for he is good..." This is followed by a repetitive antiphon at the end of each of the 26 verses, "for his steadfast love endures forever." The psalm is a litany of gratitude that is sung in a liturgical context during the Passover celebration.

The Hebrew word for loving-kindness, *hesed,* appears in all of the verses. This word refers to the enduring covenant that God has made with his people and occurs 127 times in the psalms. The psalmist brings *hesed* into the here and now in verse 23: "It is he who remembered us in our low estate, for his steadfast love endures forever" (Ps 136:23). The purpose of this psalm is to give thanks to God for *hesed,* his greatest attribute.

As is true of many of the psalms, Psalm 136 captures in poetry what other parts of the Bible state in prose, adding another layer of beauty to the telling of the story. Verses 5–9 are verses set to music to praise God for what we read about in Genesis 1:

> Who...made the heavens,
> For his steadfast love endures forever;
> Who spread out the earth on the waters,
> For his steadfast love endures forever;
> Who made the great lights,
> For his steadfast love endures forever;
> The sun to rule over the day,
> For his steadfast love endures forever;
> The moon and stars to rule over the night,
> For his steadfast love endures forever! (Ps 136:5–9)

With similar beauty, the exodus theme is captured in the poetry of verses 10–22. The basis for thanksgiving in this psalm, as for many others, is the goodness of God as experienced in the gifts of creation and redemption.

The lesson of many of the psalms is that praise and gratitude are interchangeable. I have a personal practice of praying one of the psalms every night before I go to bed. I conclude with a reflective exercise that I have found helpful in prompting me to say prayers of praise and thanks. Like many people, I have a tendency to focus on what has gone wrong rather than what has gone right during the day. For example, when I receive student evaluations of my courses, twenty-five might give excellent reviews and one might be negative. Instead of being pleased with the twenty-five positive reviews, I focus on the one negative evaluation. To change my natural tendency to focus on the negative, I spend time after praying the psalm thinking of three things that happened during the day for which I want to give praise and thanks. After each one, I repeat the phrase "for his loving-kindness endures forever." This spiritual practice has changed my life. I am now more aware of the beauty of each day, both in good moments and in difficult moments. God is present in both, for which I give thanks and praise.

For the Christian, there is added reason to give thanks and praise because of the resurrection of Jesus. We give praise because the world is created anew. All is Alleluia! The resurrection assures us that love is stronger than death, that one *plus* in the equation of life cancels out all the *minuses,* and that one tiny spark of light signals that the night is over. Because of the resurrection we can be like Zorba the Greek, the peasant in Nikos Kazantzakis' novel who is blessed with the gift of gratitude and zest for life; Zorba can dance even amidst the tragedies of this life. We can dance because Jesus Christ has won the victory over sin and death. *Alleluia* is our response and our way of life.

The Benedictine nun and author Joan Chittister writes, "What if life was meant to be one long alleluia moment?…Life itself is an exercise in learning to sing alleluia here in order to recognize the face of God hidden in the recesses of time."[11] She then goes on to propose that true joy in life comes from an ability "to deal with moments that do not feel like alleluia moments at all," and that the strength and grace to do so arise from our gratitude: "God is Good—and we know it."[12]

Gratitude is an expression of faith that celebrates life in the midst of its uncertainties and tensions. Frederich Buechner defines faith as *whistling in the dark*. Faith allows us to give thanks even when things are not well because we know that all will be well. This resonates with Julian of Norwich who says, "In all matter of things, all shall be well and all shall be well, and all manner of things shall be well."[13] It is this belief that allows us to be grateful in the midst of the struggles of life. Gratitude is a decision. It is not a feeling. Let us explore ways in which we can cultivate the practice of gratitude.

Be quick to praise and slow to condemn. Begin with what comes naturally: give thanks for the good and the beautiful. These don't have to be major events but rather the little things that happen throughout the course of the day. Say, "Thanks be to God!" as soon as you awake. Regardless of what your initial feeling might be, you are alive and you are breathing. God has given you another new morning on this earth, and who knows what surprises the day will bring. So begin by saying, "Thank you."

Once you develop this practice, you can gradually move to the next level, which is to give thanks when things do not feel good or seem beautiful. Look at these situations as opportunities for personal transformation. In fact, the greatest opportunity we have for growth is when things do not go well. We usually do not grow when we are riding the crest of the wave. It is when we are down in the dumps that we have the opportunity to deepen our dependence on God. At these moments, our prayer might be,

"God, I do not feel like giving thanks and praise, but I embrace this moment of darkness and pain as an opportunity to reach out to you and to allow you to reach out to me. I don't feel grateful but, in faith, I choose to make an act of gratitude."

This is the power in the gratitude that is prayed by the psalmist. The psalms acknowledge anger, fear, disappointment, depression, anxiety, and even despair and, yet, still summon us to prayers of gratitude. Psalm 118 is an example of a package of conflicting emotions that nevertheless conclude with praise and thanks. In one breath, we pray, "Out of my distress I called on the Lord (Ps 118:5), "All nations surrounded me" (Ps 118:10), "I was pushed hard, so that I was falling" (Ps 118:13), and end by acknowledging that God does not abandon us in these moments: "The Lord is my strength and my might; he has become my salvation" (Ps 118:14). It was for this reason that Psalm 118 was Martin Luther's favorite psalm. Luther wrote, "This is my psalm which I love…for truly it has deserved well of me many a time and has delivered me from many a sore affliction when neither the emperor nor kings nor the wise nor the cunning nor the saints were able or willing to help me."[14]

It is the practice of surprise and wonder that frees us to give thanks and praise in the midst of conflicted emotions and experiences. Life is a mystery to be lived rather than a problem to be solved. When we step back and take a deep breath in the midst of the trials and tribulations, we recognize that we are not at the center of the universe. This is the contemplative stance of the psalms, giving praise in the midst of every circumstance.

One of my first assignments as a newly ordained priest was to teach high school boys. One of the most memorable experiences from those days was my seventh-period study hall. Richard is the student whom I most fondly remember from that study hall. He would sit there each week with his elbow poised under his chin ready for sixty minutes of daydreaming. When I asked him, "What are you thinking about all during the study period?" He answered, "My girlfriend." I asked him, "How long can you think about your girlfriend?" He answered, "All day." Even though he did not know it, Richard was a contemplative who was completely absorbed in the moment. Thinking about his girlfriend filled his heart with gratitude for the gift that she was. I officiated at his wedding ten years later. Richard married the one upon whom he gazed in contemplation during his seventh-period study hall. This made for a great wedding homily!

To savor is another word for gratitude. A grateful heart embraces the moment and enjoys it. The grateful contemplative sees the preciousness of the present moment that is filled with the power of the resurrection. I recently heard a story about a deacon that illustrates my point. When it was time to pay the bills, the deacon made an act of faith and wrote out the checks even though there was not enough money in his banking account. The money arrived just in time so that his checks did not bounce. With the extra money, he took his wife out for a lobster dinner. He dipped a chunky piece of lobster in the melted butter and as he placed it in his wife's mouth said, "Taste and see the goodness of the Lord." He was inviting his wife to *savor* the joy of the moment and to join him in giving thanks.

Often when we think of prayers we think of saying words. Savoring is prayer without words. It is being caught up in the ecstasy and ordinariness of the moment. It is in this that we start to recognize that all is gift. Gradually, grateful living becomes a way of life. An example of someone who developed this practice was Felix of Cantilice, a Capuchin brother who lived in the sixteenth century. He would greet everyone with the words, "Thanks be to

God." He would say this hundreds of times each day. His veins were filled with gratitude. He refused to allow negative thoughts to live in his mind. He became a role model for the townspeople who affectionately called him Brother *Deo Gratias*.

There is a marvelous illustration of the beauty of grateful living in Michael Leach's "The Color of Gratitude." In this wonderful story, Leach writes about his wife as she struggles with Alzheimer's disease. Both Leach and his wife are blessed by the ability to appreciate the beauty of each moment together, happy for what they have rather than bitter about what they have lost. He writes, "We have a wonderful life. Every day is a good one. She is the most grateful, happy person that you'll ever meet. When we take a ride in the car, spontaneously from her lips comes, 'This is the day the Lord has made! Oh, what a beautiful day. Thank you, God.'" It is clear that Leach sees his wife as an inspiration: "She inspires me to be grateful. She lives in the present moment completely....Every day I see my job as to nurture her happiness and share in her joy. For me that's the grace of the present moment."[15]

Savoring the present moment, gratitude, and healing form a triad for our vision for living the Christian life. The German mystic John Tauler illustrates this in sharing his experience of meeting a beggar. He said to the beggar, "I hope you have a good day." The beggar replied, "Every day is a good day." Tauler asked him what he meant. He replied, "If the sun shines, I thank God; if it rains I thank God; no matter what happens I thank God." Tauler asked him, "Who are you?" He replied, "I am a king." Tauler asked, "Where is your kingdom?" He replied, "My kingdom is within me."

Yes, the kingdom is within you. You are a king or a queen— and for this reason, in the words of St. Paul, "You can give thanks always!" Not sometimes, not most of the time, but always!

THE FRUITS OF GRATEFUL LIVING

Gratitude opens our eyes to beauty in a new way. Rather than focusing on defects, gratitude opens the door to seeing beauty in all things. At a retreat that I recently gave, one of the sisters was a professional photographer. She asked if she could give one of her photographs to each retreatant. She proudly stood in front of the altar with her basket of photographs. Each person came up and randomly selected one of her treasures. I could see the joy and smiles on their faces as they looked at their gifts. At the end, I walked up to the basket, closed my eyes, and picked a photograph. When I opened my eyes, I gasped. It was a picture of a black cat with piercing black eyes. I instinctively wanted to put it back and choose another picture. This response was based on my long-held superstition that black cats were a sign of bad luck.

Since all of the retreatants were looking at me, I was embarrassed to put the picture back in the basket and exchange it for another. I was stuck with this picture that actually frightened me. After the retreat, I decided to spend time each day with the picture just looking at it and praying for a new set of eyes. After a few days, a miracle happened; what I thought was ugly suddenly became beautiful. And then I started to thank God for black cats. My attitude toward black cats began to change. Gratitude gave me an eye for beauty in places I never thought to look.

The new door that beauty opens for us creates a culture of gentleness and kindness. In the stress-filled world in which we live, we often race through life and miss most of it. Gratitude slows us down. The decision to be grateful forces us to notice what happens in every second of every day. This slowing down supports a healthier and happier lifestyle. We live in a society that affirms work and wealth, qualities that are neither good nor bad in themselves. They become bad when we make them our gods. Gratitude can transform the drudgery of the workplace into beautiful cathedrals in the mind's eye. Gratitude is contagious. As you start to see the beauty in your coworkers and in the work that needs to be done, you will begin to transform the environment. What you once saw as sterile is now beautiful. You have the capacity through gratitude to make the workplace into a garden filled with the treasures of peace, love, and joy.

Negativity is also a way of life. In fact, we can become so used to being negative that we think this is the normal way of living. We eventually begin to *become* the negative thoughts that we are thinking. Sometimes bad things happen to us that can anger or disappoint us. We can make the choice to acknowledge the negative experience and then dismiss it. A rule of thumb would be not to allow any negative thoughts or experiences to stay in your mind for more than two minutes. If they stay longer than two minutes, you're stuck and it will be difficult to break the chain of negativity.

Every human being has a dark side that prefers the darkness to the light. The seven capital sins are pride, greed, lust, gluttony, anger, envy, and laziness. To live by any one of these capital sins is to choose to live in the darkness. Gratitude is a tool that helps to bring us back into the light and away from the darkness of the capital sins. Gratitude cultivates humility (knowing that all comes from God), sharing (the desire to direct the good feelings to others), and charity (not what I can get, but what I can give). Less is more for the grateful heart. It will create peace by rejoicing in the good of others and working to make the world sacred ground made holy by grateful feet.

Gratitude is accepting life on life's terms and living it to the very fullest. Jesus promised us, "I came that they may have life, and have it abundantly" (John 10:10). Psychologists tell us that we use only 7 percent of our brainpower. If this is true, then we are *running on idle* 93 percent of the time. Negative thinking and sinful living zap the energy out of us. Grateful thinking injects joyful energy throughout the day. When you find yourself sucked in by the negative energy, respond by thanking God. This will bring you back to life and will enable you to live life far beyond the 7 percent.

GRATITUDE AS SPIRITUAL PRACTICE

Thomas Merton once wrote that he would take a *Vow of Conversation*. Borrowing from his broad interpretation of the meaning of a vow, I would propose that we take a *Vow of Gratitude*. The human person is made for gratitude. The old Catechism question was, "Why did God make us?" The answer: "God made us to know him, love him and serve him in this world and to be happy with him in the next." The happiness that God made us for begins to happen in the present moment as we love and serve him in this world. Gratitude starts here and continues into eternity. The vow of gratitude defines who we are and our mission in this world.

We need to develop creative spiritual practices to live out a vow of gratitude. The following are some suggestions on how we can make gratitude a priority in our daily lives.

- *The Gratitude Journal:* Writing as a spiritual practice is a discipline that will surprise you. When you start to write, you will tap into pockets of energy that you did not even know were there. Each day, write three things for which you are grateful. Ask yourself, "What is it about this event or experience that makes me grateful?" Try to allow the feelings to emerge. What does it feel like in this particular instance to be grateful? Give the feeling a color, a sound, and a taste. Allow the feeling to come alive. Gratitude grows out of savoring the moment. The commitment to write every day, even if just for a few minutes, will make your life blossom into a sweet bouquet that will bring beauty into your world.

- *The Rosary of Gratitude:* The rosary is an ancient form of prayer that has been adapted in a variety of forms by many religious traditions. The idea of beads and repetition of prayer is meant to be a mantra that leads you to a peaceful state of mind. It is interesting that the Church has added mysteries to think about while saying the rosary. The rosary of gratitude is not about thinking about anything. It is mindfulness in the stillness of the moment. It is difficult to stay with the silence and mindfulness. The key is to move out of your head and into your heart in the rosary of gratitude. At the end of each decade, spend two minutes giving thanks and concluding it with the words of praise, "Glory be the Father and to the Son and to the Holy Spirit. As it was in the beginning, is now, and ever shall be, world without end. Amen."

- *The Stations of Gratitude:* For each station of the cross, imagine in your mind what Jesus experienced. Try to make the event yours in the present moment. Then spend a few moments thinking of God's love for you and say, "Thank you" for the gift of this love. Conclude these moments of gratitude by asking the Lord how you might bring this gift to those you will meet today.

- *The Examen of St. Ignatius of Loyola:* The *Spiritual Exercises* of St. Ignatius are a tried and tested tool for the spiritual life. The Exercises are open to all people, men and women, young and old, cleric and lay, Catholic and non-Catholic alike. The daily *Examen*, sometimes referred to as the *Examen of Consciousness*, is a transformative spiritual practice. This exercise is meant to facilitate the Ignatian ideal of finding God in all things in the midst of the busyness of daily life. To paraphrase St. Ignatius, I would add, "Find beauty in all things." Most people like to make the *Examen* in the evening, but it can be made at any time during the day and can even be made more than once a day. There are many explanations for how to do the *Examen,* but the one that I will describe here comes from Dorothy Day. She writes about this in her journal, *The Duty of Delight.*[16]

Begin by placing yourself in God's presence. Just become aware that God is with you and you with God. You might do this with a breathing exercise: Breathe in and say each time, "God with me" and then breathe out, "Me with God." This will put you in a relaxed state, calm you down, and allow you to become aware of God's presence. Then follow the practice as Dorothy Day taught it:

Thank God for favors: Be aware of all that has happened and be lavish in your thanks to God, recognizing that all is gift.

Beg for light: Ask God to help you to see as he sees. Go back over the day with the eyes and heart of Christ, to see what really happened.

Survey: Do this almost as an old movie reel. Go through everything that has happened in the day.

Repent: Ask for forgiveness for any insensitivity to the promptings of the spirit, especially in your interactions with others.

Resolve: Ask for God's help for the next day, that you will have the grace to live it generously and joyfully and be ready to do and go wherever God calls you.

OBSTACLES TO GRATITUDE

The Spirit of God calls us to grateful living so that we can enjoy every single moment and aspect of God's creation. There are many voices that we hear every day. We need to be vigilant about those things that would draw us away from grateful living. We are competitive by nature in our society; competition is in our DNA. It is part of our human experience to compete with other people for positions in the workplace, victory in sports, and recognition of our achievements. However, competition without gratitude is about winning at all costs. A profound benefit of gratitude is that it enables us to compete while recognizing that all comes from God and that those with whom you compete are also children of God. In this context, the appropriate response for winning the prize is, "Thank you," while turning to help others along the path.

The word *Satan* in the Hebrew Scriptures means to obstruct or oppose. It is the Satan that leads you to think that the other is different from you. Thinking in this way divides the mind, heart, and the world. This will never lead to grateful living. Instead, we should follow St. Paul when he directed us, "Let the same mind be in you that was in Christ Jesus" (Phil 2:5). Sharing the attitude of Jesus Christ leads to unity rather than division.

Whenever we choose polytheism over monotheism, we will not be grateful human beings. The biggest obstacle for us is that we are often not monotheists; we worship many gods. For example, the gods of materialism, secularism, and atheism lure us to live as if God does not exist. Gratitude begins the moment we awake with our knees to the ground, thanking God and acknowledging that he is the Lord our God and there is no other. Gratitude is the way of life that he desires for you.

In his "Prayer of Thanksgiving," the Baptist theologian and social reformer Walter Rauschenbusch described the beauty of God's gifts to us, as seen with the eyes of gratitude:

> O God, we thank you for the earth, our home;
> For the wide sky and the blessed sun,
> For the salt sea and the running water,
> For the everlasting hills
> And the never-resting winds,
> For trees and the common grass underfoot.
> We thank you for our senses
> By which we hear the songs of birds,
> And see the splendor of the summer fields,
> And taste of the autumn fruits,
> And rejoice in the feel of snow,
> And smell the breath of the spring.
> Grant us a heart wide open to all this beauty;
> And save our souls from being so blind that we pass
>   unseeing
> When even the common thorn bush is aflame with
>   your glory
> O God our creator, who lives and reigns forever and ever.
>   Amen.[17]

Rauschenbusch's prayer illustrates that he has developed the art of gratitude. Read slowly and savor the prayer as an exercise in gratitude, visualizing each of the gifts that Rauschenbusch describes. Allow those images to guide you through a reflective journey of thanksgiving and praise. Reflect on the fruits of God's goodness, recognizing that gratitude and beauty enhance each other and build hope and harmony in your soul. Gratitude is an art that needs to be cultivated over a lifetime. We know we have mastered the art when our celebration of *Thanks-Giving* becomes *Thanks-Living*.

CONTINUING ON THE ROAD TO BEAUTY

1. View Bernini's sculpture *St. Teresa in Ecstasy*. What feelings do you think are going on in her in this grace-filled experience that Bernini depicts in stone? What feelings does this elicit in you? Pray with the piece and allow your heart and lips to overflow with gratitude.

2. Read Psalm 136, praying the refrain, "His loving kindness endures forever." This psalm is thanking God for Israel's salvation history. Write your own Psalm 136 that expresses your gratitude for your personal salvation history.

3. Develop a consciousness of gratitude. Be conscious and aware throughout the day of all the good that is happening in your life. Be extravagant in gratitude. Thank God and others as often as you can. Think of the people that you take for granted, such as relatives and friends.

Write a note or an email and just thank them for the gift that they are in your life.

4. Sit alone and light a candle: strike a match, light the candle, blow out the match, and enjoy the smell. Stare at the flame. Allow the candle to center you and allow the flame to bring you to that deep place within you that spills over in gratitude.

5. Read D. H. Lawrence's poem "Pax," the Latin word for peace. In this piece, he joins peace and holiness as two sides of the same coin. He invites the reader to become like a cat asleep in a chair, totally content to be with the Master. Read the poem and follow the example of the cat.

CHAPTER FIVE

DARKNESS:
THE PATH TO BEAUTY

The pain experienced in darkness often stimulates the creation of works of beauty. Pain, more often than joy, stirs creative energy in the artisans of beauty. It is the rawness of darkness that brings the human heart to new and deeper levels. John Keats, in his classic poem "Ode on Melancholy," offers a brilliant reflection on the importance of melancholy for germinating the seeds of creativity. Keats writes that melancholy "dwells with beauty" and postulates that the contrast between sadness and joy can prompt an awakening of the soul.[1]

Melancholy embodies multiple emotions, including sorrow, anger, and depression. Melancholy is the mother who births new worlds and opens new horizons to the human spirit. The dissatisfaction with things as they are is at the root of melancholy. This experience makes one feel helpless, and it brings the human spirit into the darkness that can be described as a grey cloud hovering overhead and blocking the sunlight. In the darkness, one waits for the storm to come. The natural tendency is to run from the darkness and to create a façade for the outside world. Many people react to feelings of melancholy by temporarily withdrawing from life. They miss the gift of creativity that can be found in those desert wastelands.

Melancholy carries with it a disruptive force. This force can either wake us up, prompting us to refocus our energies toward a path to light and beauty, or it can overwhelm and start us on a spiral into sorrow and hopelessness. It is our choice whether to embrace the darkness and draw strength to travel on the path toward light.

To explore the role of melancholy as a life-giving force, we return to Balthasar's pivotal reflection about Holy Saturday.[2] He believed that the Holy Saturday experience brings us closest to God. Silence, stillness, and emptiness lead us to the God of beauty. On the human journey, we are often eager to escape from the darkness of Holy Saturday to the light of Easter and the resurrection. The temptation is to leap from the drama of the passion of Good Friday to the glory of Easter Sunday. To honor the fact that we spend most of our lives in the *in between* moments of Holy Saturday is to accept the poverty of our humanity. Balthasar invites us to pause with Holy Saturday and not rush into the celebration of Easter. Holy Saturday is a melancholic day filled with more questions than answers. Balthasar suggests that we call the day *holy* because it is then that the creator-God of Genesis invites us to become co-creators.

In the William Inge play *Come Back, Little Sheba*, the characters Doc and his wife Lola respond to the onset of challenging times by clinging to thoughts of better days in the past that had been filled with promise for the future.[3] Rather than embracing the disruptive forces of melancholy as an opportunity to grow, the couple choose to dwell in the past, living what Thoreau called "lives of quiet desperation." Their Holy Saturday experience blinds them to the opportunity to become creators of beauty. Unable to progress beyond the melancholy of their Holy Saturday, they do not experience the beauty of the redemptive joy of Easter Sunday.

A pivotal life lesson is that there can be no Easter Sunday without Holy Saturday. The couple in the play is an example of what happens when the human spirit withdraws from Holy Saturday by looking for consolation in the past or the future. St. Ignatius of Loyola noted in his autobiography, "When he was thinking of the things of the world he was filled with delight, but afterward he was dry and dissatisfied. When he thought of going barefoot to Jerusalem...he was consoled...and he remained cheerful and satisfied." The emptiness of Holy Saturday eventually leads to the fullness of Easter Sunday.

Pope John Paul II was the mystic-poet. In his long poem *Easter Vigil 1966*, he writes about coming to know the God of darkness: "We stand in front of our future / Which closes and opens at the same time." His many personal experiences of Holy Saturday led him to focus on the darkness of that day as a prelude to glorious birth rather than to death: "Return to the place where a man died: return to the place / Where he was born. The past is the time of birth, not death."[4] The mystic and poet's greatest moment was as he stood at the window of the papal apartments and struggled to raise his arm in blessing one last time before returning to the Father. The window frame around him made a living portrait of the light that shines through the darkness. By living his poetry in that moment of darkness, the pope became a minister of God's beauty. For a brief moment, the world was transformed as all watched him embrace his Good Friday and Holy Saturday as he prepared to join the risen Christ in glory.

SURRENDER

We stand on holy ground when we struggle on the journey. As we resist the darkness, God invites us to surrender. A friend shared a powerful image of how she learned the power of surrender. Several years ago, she was caught in a riptide in the ocean. She struggled and was about to drown. She said that a flash of grace inspired her to give up the struggle, throw her arms back, and float. Surrender saved her life. She told me that she felt like Jacob who wrestled with an angel. When we accept the struggles in life, God can begin to take over and to lead us.

To surrender is to bless and consecrate our experience and to appreciate it for the moment of grace that it is. When we do this, we follow the example of Jesus, who made a decision to accept the Father's will. He embraced the pain of the moment in the Garden of Gethsemane, even though he struggled with conflicting emotions. God's absence coupled with the indifference of his friends brought him near despair. In the fullness of this human experience, he deepened his relationship with the Father. In utter aloneness, he surrendered, "Father,…not my will but yours be done" (Luke 22:42). In his moment of despair, Jesus created a work of beauty, an unbreakable bond with the Father. In response, the Father sent an angel to comfort him and to give him the strength to accept the cup that was given to him (John 18:11).

Charles de Foucald wrote a beautiful prayer that invites us into the Gethsemane experience. His "Prayer of Abandonment" invites us to surrender to the Father's will "without reserve and with boundless confidence." He suggests that you pray the prayer twice. The first time you pray it, imagine Jesus praying it in the garden. The second time you say it, make it your prayer.

> Father,
> I abandon myself into your hands; do with me
> what you will.
> Whatever you may do, I thank you:
> I am ready for all, I accept all.
> Let only your will be done in me, and in all
> your creatures.
> I wish no more than this, O Lord.
> Into your hands, I commend my soul;
> I offer it to you
> with all the love of my heart,
> for I love you, Lord,
> and so need to give myself,
> to surrender myself into your hands,
> without reserve,
> and with boundless confidence,
> for you are my Father.

To pray in this way, one must have the spirit of the poor, to surrender all to God. Because Jesus had this spirit, he could complete the journey that he was destined to follow. Johannes Metz believed that it is in the spirit of the poor that our transcendental neediness is nurtured, placing us on this never-ending pilgrimage from Good Friday to Easter Sunday.[5] Our daily challenge is to accept that we are all beggars on the journey. If we embrace the spiritual neediness in our hearts, we will discover that is where God lives. It is then that God fills our spirits with the riches of creative energy—if only we have the courage to give him our all.

There are multiple and conflicting energies within the human spirit that confront us in the darkness. The Greek word for these energies is *daimon*. The human heart becomes a battlefield between two spirits. One is the *daimon* of fear, which is possessive and destructive. The other is the *daimon* of love, which is generous and creative. Our spirituality is defined by the energies that we bring into the world. Whether we embark on the creative path to beauty or dive into the destructive emptiness of fear depends on what we do with the conflicting energies within the human spirit.

A SPIRITUALITY OF DARKNESS

I would propose the Carmelites St. Teresa of Avila and St. John of the Cross as mentors for a spirituality of darkness. They lived at the crossroads of the sixteenth century, a time of turmoil for the Church in the aftermath of the Protestant reformation. A spirituality was needed that would bring about individual and collective reform. Teresa and John met the challenge by reflecting on the experience of darkness in their own personal lives. From these experiences, they carved a spirituality that faced the pain of darkness as the way to reform and conversion. For example, St. Teresa wrote *The Interior Castle*, a classic about the spiritual journey.[6] She depicts God's house as a mansion with seven rooms; God lives in the inner chamber. Life is a journey that begins outside the mansion and reaches the center room, where the soul is closest to God, only when God allows that to happen. The pilgrim must have a poverty of spirit to reach the place where God waits for us all. The images of the castle and garden invite us to begin a journey that leads to beauty that exceeds our expectations. St. Teresa warns, however, that we will encounter "a mud of fear" before we reach the castle. She challenges us to wade through the mud of fear. If we persevere, we will then enter the cleansing waters of the castle and move closer to the beauty of God's love.

Teresa was the psychologist; John was the poet. His poetry describes the bittersweet experience of the spiritual journey. He wrote from personal experience; he was rejected by his brothers, who cast him into the pits of a prison cell. Like Christ, he was enveloped by darkness. The darkness of the prison cell could have made St. John a bitter man. Instead, it purified him and made him more loving. He was inspired and sustained by the crucified Christ and wrote his powerful *Spiritual Canticle* while being tortured in prison. Inspired by Christ's suffering, he produced a beautiful sketch of the crucifixion, viewing Jesus from the perspective of God above. The beautiful words over the crucifix say, *"A la tarde de la vida te examinaran en el amo"* ("In the evening of life, you will be judged on how well you loved.")

The dark night as described by the Carmelite mystics centers on the cross. The horizontal and vertical dimensions of the cross bring together the bittersweetness of earth and heaven. Jesus told us, "My yoke is easy, and my burden is light" (Matt 11:30). If individuals resolutely submit to the carrying of the cross, they will discover their pain gradually transformed into joy.

The suffering of the cross has little value in a secular culture such as ours. This is precisely why our culture needs the beauty that comes from the cross to bring it salvation. Beauty germinates in the imagination of the artist in the dark night. Creative energies emerge in the midst of the darkness when you are forced to rely on a power beyond yourself. It is here that the artist becomes a co-creator with the Creator. One needs to see in a different way in the darkness. This other mystical way of seeing is to see as the Creator sees, who "saw everything that he had made, and indeed, it was very good" (Gen 1:31). The artist begins to create what he sees and indeed it is not only good, it is beautiful.

The choice that we have is either to embrace the darkness that is the seedbed for beauty or to live in the world of mediocrity that places the inner light "under the bushel basket" (Matt 5:15). Medieval theologians described this personal inner light with the Latin word *scintilla*, the spark that lies at the heart of a person. When that inner genius blossoms and the inner spirit shines forth, mediocrity disappears. Mediocrity is a sort of dullness that prevents a person from living life fully. The contemporary spiritual writer Thomas Moore explains it well: "Dark nights of the soul play a role in transcending mediocrity. They force you to consider your situation and to feel the dark material out of which your spark arises."[7] Dark times force us to confront realities and provide opportunities to bring out the inner light.

The history of Christian spirituality testifies that darkness called people to new heights on the spiritual journey. In the first centuries of the Church, those who endured martyrdom for the sake of the faith became heroes and role models. Once Christianity became the religion of the empire, Christian blood was no longer shed. However, the desert fathers and mothers continued the theme in a new way called *white martyrdom,* in which suffering was embraced and offered up to God in acts of humility and selflessness that sought to emulate Christ. In the sixth century, St. Benedict made humility the cornerstone of his *Rule.* Humility was to be the inner journey to the desert, where one embraced the white martyrdom and drew closer to the humble beauty of Christ-like love and service to others.

All the great saints in the Christian tradition followed this path. The conversion of St. Francis of Assisi is an excellent example. Prior to his conversion, he abhorred lepers. He would run the other way when he saw a leper. After his conversion, he embraced lepers and even kissed them. St. Bonaventure in the *Legenda Maior* wrote that when St. Francis kissed the leper, it was no longer the leper who stood there but now it was Christ himself. The kiss in the mystical tradition symbolizes intimate union with God. In this instance, St. Francis experienced union with God through a dying to self that enabled him to see beyond the external ugliness of the leper. What was once repulsive to him became beautiful because he viewed it with another set of eyes. He saw the world with eyes that unveiled the presence of the Divine in all created things.

The story of St. Ignatius is similar. Like St. Francis, he had a conversion during an illness following a battle. Once he made the choice to follow Christ, his life was filled with boundless energy to share with others what was given to him. During mass, he would break into tears because he was so deeply in love with Christ. Following in the mystical path of St. Francis, he wanted to give his all to the crucified Christ. His goal was always to seek the *Magis* (the *More*) so that he might "find God in all things."

Both Francis and Ignatius were converted by embracing the cross. The Canadian Jesuit theologian Bernard Lonergan wrote that there are three levels of conversion.[8] The first is intellectual conversion, the changing of ideas; the second is moral conversion, the changing of behaviors; and the third and highest form of conversion is religious conversion, the falling in love. Love is the greatest gift that opens us up to see beauty in ourselves and to see the whole world "charged with the grandeur of God." The path to conversion begins with darkness, the dying to self that frees the soul to soar in the beauty of God's world and to fill it with love.

Mother Teresa of Calcutta gave witness in the twentieth century to the long tradition of conversion through darkness. Many were surprised, some even shocked, by her letters published after her death in a book called *Come Be My Light*.[9] Her letters to her spiritual director and friends revealed a woman who lived most of her life in darkness, tormented by an inner despair because she was unable to see God in her life. Like the Carmelite mystics before her, it was through the pain of purification that light shone through her. All of her letters describe the pain of her journey. She cries out to God to fill the emptiness in her soul, devastated by God's absence. Her honesty in these writings depicts the rawness of the suffering and feelings of abandonment that she bore so well.

I had the opportunity on several occasions to be with Mother Teresa. She radiated joy, love, and peace. Although she was close to Christ, it is evident from her letters that she did not feel that way. The grace with which Mother Teresa bore her suffering and her ability to redirect her pain into service to others and devotion to God portrays an important lesson that can help us grow closer to Christ. Often the less we feel like Christ, the more we become like Christ for others.

NAVIGATING A DARK NIGHT

"For everything there is a season, and a time for every matter under heaven" (Eccl 3:1). The world of nature teaches us that life is about seasons. We have no choice about the seasons of the human journey. What we do choose is our response to the transitions that happen to us. There are maxims that can assist us in navigating the dark nights that come with transitions.

The first maxim is *to accept life on life's terms*. To the degree that you accept the experience of the moment, you will find great peace. This requires a radical faith that can accept that God is working in the moment even when he seems to be absent. We often look at the tapestry of life from the bottom side and don't see the beauty of the piece that the Master Weaver is creating on the top side. This is a paradigm for the spiritual journey; accepting God's way is the path to life. In his poetic masterpiece "The Road Not Taken," Robert Frost describes the choice as to which road we will take in the seasons of life's transitions. The poem highlights the peace and beauty that comes from following God's plan for the transitions in life, "Two roads diverged in a wood, and I— / I took the one less traveled by, / And that has made all the difference."

As we decide what road to take, we should always look to the example of Christ. The desire to do what he did will lead us into life. The path that will lead to life is to accept the stages of life's journey, childhood to adolescence, adolescence to adulthood, adulthood to middle age, middle age to elderhood (and whatever steps there are in between). As you walk along the path, feel the darkness, the confusion, the questions, and the pain—but also smell the flowers and notice other companions on the same road. As God fed the Israelites in the desert with just enough manna for each day, so too goes the human journey; there is enough love, strength, and grace for today.

The key is to recognize that God is on the journey with you from beginning to end. The choices that you need to make, big or small, should be guided by this belief. The question you should ask for every decision and dilemma that you face is, "Which choice will deepen my relationship with God and make me a more loving human being?" Accept life on life's terms not passively but as an opportunity to take the actions that will help you to grow to the next step on your personal human faith journey.

The second maxim is *to grow deep.* You are not just moving from one stage to another on the journey. Robots and computers can store information and move along from one step to the next. We have the option of growing deeper. People sometimes use the analogy of the layers of an onion to describe the stages of life. As you peel off the layers of the onion, each layer will bring you a step deeper on the journey. Each stage will bring additional wisdom. Solomon was growing deeper when he was given the opportunity to ask for anything that he wanted and he asked for wisdom. Wisdom is seeing the connection between things; it is about integration. In J. D. Salinger's *Franny and Zooey*, Franny remarks that in the four years of college she heard the word *wisdom* used only once. In our culture, we often do not teach people how to go deeper. We scratch the surface with facts that we call knowledge. As we get older, those who make the effort to grow deeper become role models for wisdom. The mystic is the wise person who sees all as interrelated and connected. It is these people, says Rahner, to whom the future belongs.

We grow deeper and more beautiful as we age throughout the journey of life. When we are young, time seems to move slowly. For example, when we waited for Christmas as children, it seemed as though it would never arrive. As we grow older, we begin to experience time differently. For those on the spiritual journey, it is no longer *chronos,* or clock time, that determines our lives, but rather *kairos,* or graced time, that allows us to begin to experience life on God's terms. This alternative way of counting time depends on our willingness to allow the grain of wheat to die (John 12:24) so that we bear fruit as God allows it to ripen.

We begin to create a new kind of beauty as we begin to diminish physically and mentally. Itzhak Perlman is one of the greatest violinists of our time. He had polio as a very young boy, which paralyzed his legs. He walks with crutches and plays the violin from his wheelchair. In her poem "The Broken String," Grace Schulman recounts the incident when Perlman was playing the violin at a concert filled with hundreds of people and one of the strings snapped. There was an audible gasp from the audience and, after a few seconds that seemed like an eternity, Perlman motioned for the conductor to continue. He finished the performance with only three strings on his violin. There was not a dry eye in the place as the audience offered enthusiastic applause that went on for close to five minutes. Perlman then stood before the crowd and said, "This has been my vocation, my lifelong mission—to make music out of what remains."[10] In that moment, Perlman became a work of beauty with the power to transform the world. "To make music out of what is broken" is the vocation given to us as we experience strength through weakness in the transitions of life.

I understood this truth in a new and deeper way during a recollection day I recently gave for senior priests and religious. Their clouded eyes, wrinkled faces, and limping bodies were a living gospel. As they formed the communion line, I was overwhelmed by the procession of broken strings, the saints coming forward as they sang, "Take, Lord, Receive." These sisters and priests continued to give their all in the winter of life. In his book *The Divine Milieu*, the French philosopher Teilhard de Chardin wrote powerfully about what it means to grow deeper as we grow older. In this piece, he acknowledges feeling sorrow at the weakening of his body as he approaches the end of his life. He contrasts his frailty with the power of God, who will sustain him through the end of his journey on earth. Praying for grace, he writes, "It is not enough that I should die while communicating. Teach me to communicate while dying."[11]

The third maxim is *to remember that there is a sense in humor.* In the midst of the dark night, an important quality to cultivate is a sense of humor. Native Americans have a beautiful tradition for choosing the godparents of newly born babies. The first person who makes a baby smile becomes the godparent for the baby. They believe that it is in that moment of laughter that the Spirit enters the soul of the newborn. The wise ones in this tradition are those who smile, those who have a sense of humor in the midst of the trials and tribulations of daily life.

Being in touch with works of beauty helps one to see the larger picture and brings joy even in the midst of sadness. Music, film, and art often portray this message. For example, hymns like "Amazing Grace" touch people's hearts and get them through tough moments. Films like *It's a Wonderful Life* tap into the deep sorrow that gradually brings about joy. This joy is not a superficial laughter that covers pain and can be a form of denial. In fact, this spiritual joy does not depend on external circumstances but rather is based on a profound belief that ultimately "all things work together for good for those who love God" (Rom 8:28).

Beauty heals us and offers a different perspective, one that opens our eyes to joy. Steve Jobs intuited that people needed to experience beauty even in technology.[12] In creating the Apple products, his goal was to create works of beauty that would move people away from fear of a machine to a sense of awe as they experienced new technologies. In an address he gave to the students at Stanford University after he was diagnosed with cancer, he told them that the most important thing to do in life is to embrace the fact that you are going to die. If you do this, then you will recognize what is important and dismiss what is trivial. You will live each moment to the fullest. As he lay dying, Jobs gave last loving glances to his wife, children, and sister and, then, looked beyond them and, whatever or whomever he saw, his last words were "O Wow, O Wow, O Wow!" He now beheld the One who makes all things new.

As we experience the dark nights of life, it is easy to lose the vision of Jesus Christ, the One who is the beginning and the end of the journey. The temptations of Christ in the desert described in Matthew 4 are paradigms for the issues that are roadblocks on the journey and can make us lose our way, our vision. The temptation to turn stones into bread was the temptation to use power for one's own benefit. The temptation to kneel before Satan and to be given the kingdoms of the world was the temptation to seek status for self-interest. The temptation to throw himself from the mountain and let the angels catch him was the temptation to give up responsibility for his life. If we stumble in the face of our temptations, God always invites us to get up and start over again.

The temptations of life can dampen and sour the human spirit. Humor is a positive tool that can be used in the midst of temptations. To be able to laugh in the face of the devil means that you see the incongruity of it all. You can accept the mystery of life and recognize that life is not a problem to be solved but rather a mystery to be lived. It enables you to say, "no" to anything that is not life giving and to say, "yes" to life as it is.

As Mother Teresa suffered, she still smiled. She said, "I can do only one thing, like a little dog follow closely the Master's footsteps. Pray that I be a cheerful dog."[13] She committed herself to becoming an *apostle of joy* instead of wallowing in her misery. She faced every day, with its joys and sorrows, uncertainties and consolations, always with a smile, one that was not artificial but one that came from her confidence that "I know that my Redeemer lives!" (Job 19:25).

EXPERTS IN COMPASSION

The Benedictine Abbot Dom Chapman, in his spiritual letters, suggested that the relationship between contemplation and
charity must be seamless. He writes, "One must accept joyfully and
with the whole will exactly the state of prayer which God makes
possible for us here and now; we will to have that, and no other. It
is just what God wills for us."[14] Chapman proposes that we pay less
attention to *methods* in prayer and more attention to *charity*. The
charity in our lives is the surest sign that our prayer is authentic and
that our lives are moving in the right direction.

Compassion is an expression of charity, which is the greatest
gift (1 Cor 13:13). It is precisely in the darkness that the God who
is love teaches us how to be compassionate, to *suffer with*. Empathy
is to feel the pain of another. Sympathy is to enter into the pain of
another. Both of these words are found in psychological manuals.
You will not find the word *compassion* in these manuals. When you
look up the word, you will find that it is defined as "a religious
word." Compassion flows from depths of a faith that pulsates
within the human heart. If there is one word that defines the life
and ministry of Jesus Christ, that word is *compassion*. His is compassion for the poor, the sick, the marginalized, and the forgotten.
He is the good shepherd who reaches out for the lost sheep. The
mysticism of darkness that leads to compassionate hearts is best
described in Matthew 25. Feeding the hungry, giving drink to the
thirsty, visiting the imprisoned, clothing the naked are what define
the life of the Christian. Heaven is to focus on others, to become
absorbed in the world; hell is to be absorbed in self. The way of
compassion is one in which our sisters and brothers become sacraments of God's hidden presence among us.

The compassion of Mother Teresa epitomized the beauty that is found in giving oneself to others. She told a wonderful story about an Aborigine that she met while caring for the poor in Australia.[15] The man was old and lonely and living in a tin shack on the reservation. Mother Teresa cleaned his hut for him and uncovered a beautiful lantern that was never used. She gently convinced him to light the lamp to welcome the visiting sisters, opening a ray of beauty in his life that was never extinguished. Two years later, he told one of the nuns, "Tell Mother, my friend, the light she lit in my life is still burning."

The beautiful light that comes out of the darkness is the light of compassion. The goal of the spiritual life is our transformation through darkness into experts in compassion. This compassion for others as we follow Christ is the most profound work of beauty that humans can create. As we live our lives in the hectic and sometimes confusing seasons of our contemporary world, we must remember always to nurture the beauty of Christian spirituality in our souls and let that light shine on those around us. This spiritual practice will ground us in eternal truths that will fill our spirits with God's grace in the twenty-first century, just as they have since the beginning of time. Beauty will transform the world because beauty transforms human hearts.

CONTINUING ON THE ROAD TO BEAUTY

1. Western art historically has placed an emphasis on Christ's agony and suffering. In contrast, the eleventh-century Eastern icon that has been named the San Damiano Crucifix stresses Christ's freedom and the gift

that he makes of himself. It is called the San Damiano Crucifix because it was in that church that this crucifix spoke to St. Francis of Assisi in 1206, asking him to "Rebuild my Church." Allow this magnificent icon to look at you and to speak to your heart.

2. View the crucifix drawn by St. John of the Cross and the Salvador Dali painting inspired by the sketch. In the darkness, St. John created a work of beauty. What thoughts, memories, and feelings about periods of darkness in your life does this elicit in you? What beauty or creative energies came out of the darkness in your life?

3. Reflect on these words by the Buddhist monk Thich Nhat Hahn:

A beautiful rose we have just cut and placed in our vase is immaculate. It smells so good, so pure, so fresh...The opposite is a garbage can. It smells horrible, and it is filled with rotten things. But that is only when you look on the surface. If you look more deeply, you will see that in just five or six days, the rose will become part of the garbage. You do not need to wait five days to see it. If you just look at the rose, and you look deeply, you can see it now. And if you look into the garbage can, you can see that in a few months its contents can be transformed into lovely vegetables, and even a rose... Looking at the rose you can see the garbage, and looking at the garbage you can see the rose. Roses and garbage inter-are. Without a rose, we cannot have garbage; and without garbage, we cannot have a rose. They need each other very much. The rose and the garbage are equal. The garbage is just as precious as the rose.[16]

Think about the interchange between *roses* and *garbage* in your life.

4. Make the Stations of the Cross or read the Passion narratives in one of the Gospels. Try to get into the darkness, the pain, and the agony of Jesus to deepen your understanding of what he experienced.

5. View the *Transfiguration* icon by Protodeacon Paul Hommes and read the transfiguration account in one of the Gospels. Can you identify with Peter, James, and John in their desire to build three tents and stay there? In what ways do transfiguration experiences prepare us for darkness, entering into the dying of Christ so that we might rise with him?

A CONCLUSION
TO BEAUTY

A spirituality of beauty serves a pressing need for the twenty-first century as it offers an alternative to the values of contemporary culture. We live in a time when society has defined beauty to meet its characterization of success. Our culture focuses predominantly on physical beauty and its role in promoting success in the competitive environment of our society. This philosophy carries its own message about who and what are beautiful and encourages a utilitarian and oftentimes superficial view of beauty.

A great deal has been written about the values associated with beauty in recent years. Many of these studies are based on social-science methodologies that explain how physical beauty can make a difference in the marketplace. The studies illustrate the contemporary bias that human beauty is based exclusively on external factors, such as age, weight, height, race, and gender.[1] As we have seen in this book, such a limited definition of beauty misses the opportunity to connect to a spirituality that is lifted on the wings of the fundamental beauty of our existence.

If for no other reason, we need to craft a spirituality of beauty to offer an alternative to these destructive and demoralizing cultural norms. A spirituality of beauty summons the human spirit to look beyond the surface to a deeper consciousness to discover God's version of beauty. As opposed to the values of today's society, which often reduce beauty to that which is practical or superficial, we need a spirituality of beauty that dares to transcend practicality in the eyes of the world because it cannot be measured by secular standards. This spirituality of beauty would draw its standards from those of the Creator, who saw all that he has made not only as good but also as beautiful.

In the preceding chapters, we have encountered alternative definitions of beauty that are broader and deeper than the transient values of today's culture. There is something *ever ancient, ever new* about this perspective on beauty that resonates with the quest for spirituality in the twenty-first century. You might ask, "What is new and not-so-new about a spirituality of beauty?" There is nothing new about the quest for God, about reaching out to the transcendent; the "I want spirituality" mantra of our culture is ever ancient. In developing a perspective on the spirituality of beauty that is relevant to the twenty-first century, I have reached into the attics and cellars of the Christian tradition. I have pulled out some concepts that have been in storage, dusted them off, and repackaged them for our times. What is new about this spirituality is its attempt to reclaim the primacy of beauty that has been forgotten on a back shelf for too long a time. Viewing the staples of the Christian tradition, such as gratitude and forgiveness, through the lens of beauty provides a spirituality of beauty that is *ever new* with respect to the contemporary values of the society in which we live, and, yet, *ever ancient* in a way that is inherently familiar to our deepest souls.

The spirituality of beauty presented here is an effort to fill a void in our contemporary culture and religion. Not only has the culture failed to satisfy the human spirit with its approach to beauty but so also has religion. Balthasar's observation that beauty is the most neglected attribute of God in modern theology prompted him to write his theological aesthetics.[2] At the center of his theology is a very basic truth: in the incarnation, God has transformed the very essence of culture. Balthasar's theological vision is "to reintegrate grace and nature, thought and feeling, body and mind, culture and theology within a synthetic comprehensive, theological reflection on form."[3] The foundation of Balthasar's theology of beauty is that God is the Beautiful One, who loves us so much that he comes into the darkness of chaos, hate, and ugliness to pull the human spirit into the sphere of divine beauty. This concept not only restores beauty as an attribute of God; it also reclaims the human person as a reflection of God's beauty.

I believe it was the loss of emphasis on the place of beauty in spirituality that prompted the Council fathers to address artists at the conclusion of the Second Vatican Council on December 8, 1965. In this address, Pope Paul VI said that friends of genuine art are friends of the Church. He told the artists, "It is beauty...which brings joy to the heart of man...and all of this is done through your hands....Remember that you are the guardians of beauty in the world. May that suffice to free you from tastes that are passing."

Pope John Paul II further developed the themes addressed to artists at the conclusion of the Council in his *Letter to Artists*, which we turn to many times in this book for its clarity in defining the role of beauty in supporting one's spiritual life. It was to celebrate the tenth anniversary of Pope John Paul's letter that Pope Benedict XVI met with over two hundred artists from around the world beneath Michelangelo's fresco of *The Last Judgment* in the Sistine Chapel. He urged them to be heralds and witnesses of hope for humanity and not to be afraid to enter into dialogue with believers who also see themselves as pilgrims on a journey toward infinite beauty and glory. Commenting on the fresco, he said to the artists, "*The Last Judgment* which you see behind me reminds us that human history is movement and ascent, a continuing tension towards fullness, toward human happiness, toward a horizon that always transcends the present moment as the two coincide."

A spirituality of beauty discovers its ultimate goal in the vision of Michelangelo's fresco. The God who created this beautiful world will bring it to a grace-filled completion at the end of time. It is beauty that sustains and motivates us as we live in this in-between time. Beauty is our roadmap that nudges us to see new manifestations of the Divine each day as we journey back to the kingdom. The spirituality presented in these pages presents beauty as a way of seeing that can only be fully appreciated when experienced in the present moment. Once healed from the blindness caused by life's hurts by accepting and offering forgiveness, we can then come back to the beauty of the present moment. It is in this sacred meeting that the human spirit is filled with gratitude. The raw material for this synthesis arises from the darkness of the chaos of life where the Spirit of God makes us into a new creation.

We have a powerful illustration of the inner dynamic of this spirituality in the experience of Beethoven. It was during a time of great personal turmoil that Ludwig van Beethoven composed his Symphony No. 2 in D major. He had become despondent about the deterioration of his hearing, to the point that he confided the secret and the pain that it caused him to his friend Franz Wegeler. It was through his experience of despondency that Beethoven was able to produce one of his happiest works, from which he received consolation and touched the spirits of millions of people over time. During the process of grieving, Beethoven not only created a work of beauty, he became a work of beauty. By staying in the present moment and confronting the darkness of his situation, he was recreated. He was filled with a gratitude for his gifts that energized him to become a co-creator of beauty that has brought joy and beauty to the multitudes.

Every experience of beauty has the potential of placing us in touch with the transcendent. The Israelites articulated this belief in Psalm 27 as they prayed, "One thing I asked of the Lord, that will I seek after: to live in the house of the Lord all the days of my life, to behold the beauty of the Lord, and to inquire in his temple" (Ps 27:4). The psalmist captures a profound theological principle that the fundamental human desire is to "behold the beauty of the Lord." This gets to the heart of the matter. God is not only beautiful; God is beauty. We come to know God's beauty by experiencing the fruits of God's creative activity. The beauty of the world is God's handiwork. Balthasar says it in this way, "The cosmos is experienced as the representation and manifestation of the hidden transcendent beauty of God, since God in creating the world, does not only give it being but also imparts his own qualities in it so that it bears some likeness to him."[4] Balthasar recaptures the tradition of the Eastern fathers who taught that God is not only beauty itself but that all beauty stems from the One who is all-beautiful. This is the basis of the sacramental principle that all beauty is mediated in the context of the material world. Although artists create works of beauty for us, we are all called to be artisans of God's beauty by our lives, words, and actions in the world.

We become artisans of God's beauty when we recognize the face of God in our neighbors and ourselves. In the final act of Thornton Wilder's play *Our Town*, Emily, a young mother that we saw grow up in the play, has just been buried. Before going to the next life, she asks to return to earth for "just one moment." She is told that she can, but to "choose the least important day in your life. It will be important enough." What is implied is that every day is important. As Emily relives the moment of waking up on her twelfth birthday, she cries out, "It goes so fast. We don't have time to look at one another....Oh earth, you are too wonderful for anybody to realize you." She asks the stage manager, "Do any human beings ever realize life while they live it—every, every minute?" And the stage manager responds, "No. The saints and the poets, maybe they do some."[5]

A spirituality of beauty invites us to become saints and poets who recognize the One who is Beauty on the ordinary Emmaus road of everyday life. "Then their eyes were opened, and they recognized him; and he vanished from their sight. They said to each other, 'Were not our hearts burning within us while he was talking to us on the road?'" (Luke 24:31–32). The conclusion to beauty is again a new beginning, as you become a community of the beautiful. May your hearts burn within you while you talk with him and with one another on the road.

NOTES

Introduction

1. John E. Rotelle, ed., *The Confessions of St. Augustine,* bk. 10, trans. Maria Boulding (Hyde Park, NY: New City Press, 1997), 262.

2. Fyodor Dostoyevsky, *The Idiot,* trans. Constance Garnett (New York: The Heritage Press, 1956), 346.

3. Adam Mickiewicz, "Oda do mlodosci," in *Wybór poezji,* v. 69 (Wroclaw, 1986), 1:63.

4. Evelyn Underhill, *Mysticism: A Study of the Nature and Development of Man's Spiritual Consciousness* (New York: E. P. Dutton, 1912), 117.

Chapter 1

1. Many documents and works of art referred to in this book are listed at the back of the book in "Web Site References," which gives an online Web address at which the work can be viewed or read online.

2. *Wizard of Oz*, Victor Fleming, director (MGM Studios, 1939).

3. Bernard Lonergan, *Insight: A Study of Human Understanding*, vol. 2, Collected works of Bernard Lonergan, Frederick E. Crowe and Robert M. Doran, eds. (Toronto: University of Toronto Press, 1957), 212.

4. Albert Camus, *Create Dangerously,* Lecture at the University of Uppsala in Sweden, December 14, 1957.

5. Hans Urs von Balthasar, *The Glory of the Lord: A Theological Aesthetics,* Joseph Fessio and John Riches, eds. (Edinburgh: T&T Clark, 1982–1989).

6. Gerard Manley Hopkins, "God's Grandeur," *Gerard Manley Hopkins: The Major Works*, ed. Catherine Phillips (Oxford: Oxford University Press, 1986, 2002), 128.

7. Rotelle, *Confessions of St. Augustine*, 262 (see intro., n. 1).

8. Ibid., bk. 1, 16.

9. Alice Walker, *The Color Purple* (New York: Simon & Schuster, 1982), 191.

10. Georges Bernanos, *Diary of a Country Priest* (New York: Carroll and Graf, 2002), 298.

Chapter 2

1. Thomas Friedman, *The Lexus and the Olive Tree: Understanding Globalization* (New York: Farrar, Straus & Giroux, 1999), 23.

2. Robert Bly, *Kabir: Ecstatic Poems* (Boston: Beacon Press, 2004), 17.

3. Maya Angelou, *On the Pulse of Morning* (New York: Random House, 1993).

4. Ann Wilson Schaef and Diane Fassel, *The Addictive Organization* (San Francisco: Harper & Row, 1988).

5. New Roman Missal (Chicago: Archdiocese Liturgical Training Program, 2011), 665.

6. Jean-Pierre de Caussade, *Abandonment to Divine Providence* (New York: Image Books/Doubleday), 36.

7. Ibid., 91.

8. Robert McAfee Brown, ed., *The Essential Reinhold Niebuhr: Selected Essays and Addresses* (New Haven, CT: Yale University Press, 1987), 251.

9. Anthony Ciorra and James Keating, *Moral Formation in the Parish* (New York: Alba House, 1998), 42–46.

10. St. Francis of Assisi and St. Clare, *The Canticle of Brother Sun*, trans. Regis Armstrong and Ignatius Brady (New York: Paulist Press, 1982), 37.

11. Kabir, "The Time Before Death," in *Ten Poems to Change Your Life*, ed. Robert Houston (New York: Harmony, 2001), 53.

12. St. Catherine of Siena, http://www.stcatherine-ml.org/About/Patron.htm.

13. Ciorra, *Moral Formation*, 37.

14. de Caussade, *Abandonment*, 57.

15. de Caussade, *Abandonment*, 52.

16. Samuel Taylor Coleridge, *Bibliographia Literaria: Or, Biographical Sketches of My Literary Life and Opinions* (1817), chap. 14.

17. Stephen Greenblatt and others, eds., *The Norton Shakespeare*, 2nd ed. (New York: W. W. Norton, 2008), 2415.

18. Jürgen Moltmann, *God in Creation: A New Theology of Creation and the Spirit of God*, trans. Margaret Kohl (Minneapolis: Fortress Press, 1993), 307.

19. James Joyce, *A Portrait of the Artist as A Young Man* (New York: Random House, The Modern Library, 1928), 249.

Chapter 3

1. Charles J. Robinson, "Known," *Duke Divinity School Review* 44 (1979): 44.

2. Patricia Maxwell Lewis, "The Cost of Grace," *The Tablet* 4823 (April 8, 2006): 4–5.

3. Camille D'Arienzo, "Mercy Toward Our Fathers," *America* 199 (August 18, 2008), http://www.americamagazine.org/content/article.cfm?article_id=10970.

4. Ibid.

5. "Easter Vigil," in New Roman Missal (Chicago: Archdiocese Liturgical Training Program, 2011), 199.

6. Rene Girard, "The Scapegoat and Myths as Texts of Persecution," in *The Girard Reader*, James G. Williams, ed. (Crossroad, NY: Crossroad Herder, 1996), 97–144.

7. Fyodor Dostoyevsky, *The Brothers Karamazov*, trans. Richard Pevear and Larissa Volokhonsky (New York: Vintage, 1991), 58.

8. *The Twelve Steps and the Twelve Traditions* (New York: Alcoholic Anonymous World Services, 1965).

9. "Common Preface IV," in New Roman Missal (Chicago: Archdiocese Liturgical Training Program, 2011), 468.

10. Karl Rahner, "Reflections on the Experience of Grace," *Theological Investigations,* vol. 3 (London: Helicon Press, 1967), 86–90.

11. St. Francis of Assisi, *Canticle of Brother Sun*, 37 (see chap. 2, n. 10).

12. Ibid.

13. Alex Garcia-Rivera, *A Wounded Innocence: Sketches for a Theology of Art* (Collegeville, MN: Liturgical Press, 2003), 90.

Chapter 4

1. William J. Young, ed. and trans., *Letters of St Ignatius of Loyola* (Chicago: Loyola UP, 1959), 55.

2. Leon Joseph Cardinal Suenens, *A New Pentecost* (New York: Seabury Press, 1974).

3. G. K. Chesterton, *St. Francis of Assisi* (New York: Doran, 1924), 114.

4. Suenens, *New Pentecost.*

5. Leon Joseph Suenens, *The Critic* (November 1970), cover.

6. St. Anselm, *Cur Deus Homo*, trans. Sydney Norton Deane (Chicago: Open Court Publishing, 1903).

7. C. S. Lewis, *The Problem of Pain* (San Francisco: HarperCollins, 2001), 130.

8. Hans Urs von Balthasar, *The von Balthasar Reader*, ed. Medard Kehl and Werner Loser, trans. Robert J. Daly and Fred Lawrence (New York: Crossroad, 1982), 110.

9. Ibid., 114.

10. Ibid., 115.

11. Joan Chittister and Rowan Williams, *Uncommon Gratitude: Alleluia for All That Is* (Collegeville, MN: Liturgical Press, 2010), viii–ix.

12. Ibid.

13. *Julian of Norwich: Showings*, trans. Edward Colledge and James Walsh, Classics of Western Spirituality (New York: Paulist Press, 1978), 229.

14. Arthur Weiser, "The Psalms," in *Old Testament Library (Commentary)* (Philadelphia: Westminster Press, 1962), 723–4.

15. Michael Leach, "The Color of Gratitude," *The National Catholic Reporter* 47 (2011): 3a.

16. Dorothy Day, *The Duty of Delight: The Diaries of Dorothy Day*, ed. Robert Ellsberg (Milwaukee: Marquette University Press, 2008), 129–30.

17. Walter Rauschenbusch, *Prayers of the Social Awakening* (Boston, New York, and Chicago: The Pilgrim Press, 1910), 47.

Chapter 5

1. John Keats, "Ode on Melancholy," in *The Oxford Book of English Verse,* ed. Arthur Thomas Quiller-Couch (Oxford: Clarendon, 1919), [c1901]; Bartleby.com, www.bartleby.com/101/ (accessed July 15, 2012).

2. von Balthasar, *von Balthasar Reader*, 110 (see chap. 4, n. 8).

3. William Inge, *Come Back, Little Sheba* (London: Samuel French, 1978).

4. Karol Wojtyla, *Easter Vigil and Other Poems*, trans. Jerzy Peterkiewicz (New York: Random House, 1979), 76.

5. Johannes Baptist Metz, *Poverty of Spirit*, trans. John Drury (New Jersey: Newman Press, 1968), 28–29.

6. St. Teresa of Avila, *Interior Castle*, ed. and trans. Allison Peers (New York: Doubleday, 1961).

7. Thomas Moore, *Dark Nights of the Soul: A Guide to Finding Your Way Through Life's Ordeals* (New York: Gotham, 2004), 312–13.

8. Bernard Lonergan, *Early Works on the Theological Method I*, vol. 22, Collected Works of Bernard Lonergan, ed. Robert M. Doran and Robert C. Croken (Toronto: University of Toronto Press, 1988).

9. Mother Teresa and Brian Kolodiejchuk, *Come Be My Light: The Private Writings of the Saint of Calcutta* (New York: Doubleday, 2007).

10. Grace Schukman, "The Broken String," in *The Broken String: Poems* (New York: Houghton Mifflin, 2007), 3.

11. Pierre Teilhard de Chardin, *Divine Milieu: An Essay on the Interior Life* (New York: Harper, 1960), 62–63.

12. Walter Isaacson, *Steve Jobs* (New York: Simon & Schuster, 2011).

13. Mother Teresa, *Come Be My Light*, 236.

14. John Chapman, *Spiritual Letters* (New York: Continuum, 2003), 294.

15. Mother Teresa, *Come Be My Light*, 339–40.

16. Thich Nhat Hanh, *Essential Writings*, Modern Spiritual Masters Series, ed. Robert Ellsberg (Maryknoll, NY: Orbis Books, 2008), 56–57.

Conclusion

1. Daniel S. Hamermesh, *Beauty Pays: Why Attractive People are More Successful* (New Jersey: Princeton University Press, 2011); Catherine Hakim, *Erotic Capital: The Power of Attraction in the Boardroom and the Bedroom* (Philadelphia: Basic Books, 2011).

2. Hans Urs von Balthasar, *Word and Revelation: Essays in Theology I* (New York: Herder and Herder, 1964), 162.

3. Louis Dupre, "The Glory of the Lord: Hans Urs von Balthasar's Theological Aesthetics," *Communion* XVI (1989): 386.

4. von Balthasar, *Glory of the Lord*, vol. 1, 154 (see chap. 1, n. 5).

5. Thornton Wilder, *Our Town* (New York: HarperCollins, 2003), 106–8.

Web Site References

Introduction

VATICAN DOCUMENTS

Pope John Paul II, *Letter to Artists*, 1999, http://www.vatican.va/
holy_father/john_paul_ii/letters/documents/hf_jp-ii_
let_23041999_artists_en.html

Pope Paul VI, *Address of Pope Paul VI to Artists,* December 8, 1965,
http://www.vatican.va/holy_father/paul_vi/speeches/1965
/documents/hf_p-vi_spe_19651208_epilogo-concilio-
artisti_en.html

POETIC AND OTHER TEXTS

Alexandr Solzhenitsyn, Nobel Lecture (1970), http://www.nobel-prize.org/nobel_prizes/literature/laureates/1970/solzhenit-syn-lecture.html

Chapter 1

VATICAN DOCUMENTS

Pope Benedict XVI, apostolic exhortation *Verbum Domini*, http://www.vatican.va/holy_father/benedict_xvi/apost_exhortations/documents/hf_ben-xvi_exh_20100930_verbum-domini_en.html

Pope Benedict XVI, *Art and Prayer*, August 31, 2011, http://www.vatican.va/holy_father/benedict_xvi/audiences/2011/documents/hf_ben-xvi_aud_20110831_en.html

Pope John Paul II, *Letter to Artists*, 1999, http://www.vatican.va/holy_father/john_paul_ii/letters/documents/hf_jp-ii_let_23041999_artists_en.html

Pope Paul VI, *Speech to Artists*, May 7, 1964, http://www.vatican.va/holy_father/paul_vi/homilies/documents/hf_p-vi_hom_19640507_messa-artisti_it.html (given in Italian only)

Second Vatican Council, *Constitution on the Church in the Modern World*, http://www.vatican.va/archive/hist_councils/ii_vatican_council/documents/vat-ii_const_19651207_gaudium-et-spes_en.html

POETIC AND OTHER TEXTS

St. Basil, *Homily on Psalm 29*, www.scribd.com/doc/39119076/St-Basil-the-Great-Exegetic-Homilies, 213

T. S. Eliot, "The Naming of Cats," http://allpoetry.com/poem/ 8453755-The_Naming_Of_Cats-by-T_S_Eliot

Gerard Manley Hopkins, "God's Grandeur," http://www.bartleby. com/122/7.html

VISUAL WORKS OF ART

Ansel Adams, *Oak Tree, Sunrise,* http://www.chooseart.net/ansel_ adams.html

Claude Monet, *Poplars,* http://en.wikipedia.org/wiki/Poplar_ Series_(Monet)

Rembrandt, *Self-Portrait as the Apostle Paul,* http://www.mystudios .com/rembrandt/rembrandt-scenes-apostle-paul.html

Rembrandt, *The Return of the Prodigal Son,* http://www.wikipaintings .org/en/rembrandt/the-return-of-the-prodigal-son-1669

Chapter 2

POETIC AND OTHER TEXTS

T. S. Eliot, *Ash-Wednesday,* http://www.msgr.ca/msgr-7/ash_ wednesday_t_s_eliot.htm

Gerard Manley Hopkins, "Pied Beauty," http://www.bartleby.com /122/13.html

Robert Morneau, "Fiat," http://predmore.blogspot.com/2010/03/ poem-fiat-by-robert-fr-morneau.html

Orthodox Prayer for Nativity Vespers, http://www.incommunion .org/2004/12/13/rescued-by-christmas

VISUAL WORKS OF ART

Convent of San Marco, Florence, Reproductions of frescos, http://www.museumsinflorence.com/musei/museum_of_ san_marco.html

Convent of San Marco, Florence, Virtual tour, http://www.
    youtube.com/watch?v=aGsm2p4cLP0

Ode to Joy Flash Mob, Barcelona, http://www.youtube.com/
    watch?feature=prayer_embedded&v=GBaHPND2QJg

Andrei Rublev, Icon of the Holy Trinity, http://www.holy-
    transfiguration.org/library_en/lord_trinity_rublev.html

Henry O. Tanner, *Annunciation*, http://www.americamagazine
    .org/content/article.cfm?article_id=10719

Novgorod School, Icon of the Nativity, http://www.hermitage
    museum.org/html_En/04/b2003/hm4_1_o_0.html

Chapter 3

POETIC AND OTHER TEXTS

St. Francis of Assisi, "Canticle of the Creatures," http://www.
    appleseeds.org/canticle.htm

VISUAL WORKS OF ART

Rembrandt, *The Return of the Prodigal Son,* http://www.wikipaintings.
    org/en/rembrandt/the-return-of-the-prodigal-son-1669

Chapter 4

POETIC AND OTHER TEXTS

D. H. Lawrence, "Pax," http://www.gratefulness.org/poetry/after_
    meditation.htm

VISUAL WORKS OF ART

Bernini, *St. Teresa in Ecstasy*, http://en.wikipedia.org/wiki/
    File:Estasi_di_Santa_Teresa.jpg

William Holman Hunt, *The Light of the World*, http://
londonbygaslight.wordpress.com/2012/07/11/local-
victoriana-light-of-the-world/

Chapter 5

POETIC AND OTHER TEXTS

Charles de Foucauld, "Prayer of Abandonment," http://www.
crossroadsinitiative.com/library_article/212/Prayer_of_
Abandonment__Charles_de_Foucauld.html

Robert Frost, "The Road Not Taken," www.bartleby.com/119/
1.html

Gerard Manley Hopkins, "God's Grandeur," www.bartleby.com/122

Ignatius Loyola, *The Autobiography of St. Ignatius*, http://www.
gutenberg.org/ebooks/24534

Henry David Thoreau, *Walden*, http://www.gutenberg.org/
catalog/world/readfile?fk_files=2121329&pageno=5

VISUAL WORKS OF ART

Salvador Dali, *Christ of St. John of the Cross*, http://en.wikipedia
.org/wiki/Christ_of_Saint_John_of_the_Cross

Paul Hommes, *Transfiguration*, http://www.flickr.com/photos
/jimforest/5995170874/

San Damiano Crucifix, http://en.wikipedia.org/wiki/San_
Damiano_cross

Conclusion

VATICAN DOCUMENTS

Pope Benedict XVI, *Art and Prayer*, August 31, 2011, http://www.
vatican.va/holy_father/benedict_xvi/audiences/2011/
documents/hf_ben-xvi_aud_20110831_en.html

Pope Paul VI, *Address of Pope Paul VI to Artists,* December 8, 1965, http://www.vatican.va/holy_father/paul_vi/speeches/1965 /documents/hf_p-vi_spe_19651208_epilogo-concilio-artisti_en.html

Pope John Paul II, *Letter to Artists,* 1999, http://www.vatican.va/ holy_father/john_paul_ii/letters/documents/hf_jp-ii_ let_23041999_artists_en.html